AF642153

ARRIVAL

21ST CENTURY FILM ESSENTIALS

Cinema has a storied history, but its story is far from over. 21st Century Film Essentials offers a lively chronicle of cinema's second century, examining the landmark films of our ever-changing moment. Each book makes a case for the importance of a particular contemporary film for artistic, historical, or commercial reasons. The twenty-first century has already been a time of tremendous change in filmmaking the world over, from the rise of digital production and the ascent of the multinational blockbuster to increased vitality in independent filmmaking and the emergence of new voices and talents both on screen and off. The films examined here are the ones that embody and exemplify these changes, crystallizing emerging trends or pointing in new directions. At the same time, they are films that are informed by and help refigure the cinematic legacy of the previous century, showing how film's past is constantly reimagined and rewritten by its present. These are films both familiar and obscure, foreign and domestic; they are new but of lasting value. This series is a study of film history in the making. It is meant to provide a different kind of approach to cinema's story—one written in the present tense.

Donna Kornhaber, *Series Editor*

ALSO IN THE SERIES

Noah Tsika, *I'm Not There*
Scott Bukatman, *Black Panther*
J. J. Murphy, *The Florida Project*
Patrick Keating, *Harry Potter and the Prisoner of Azkaban*
Dana Polan, *The LEGO Movie*

Arrival

David Roche

UNIVERSITY OF TEXAS PRESS AUSTIN

Copyright © 2024 by the University of Texas Press
All rights reserved
Printed in the United States of America
First edition, 2024

Requests for permission to reproduce material from this work should be sent to permissions@utpress.utexas.edu.

♾ The paper used in this book meets the minimum requirements of ANSI/NISO Z39.48-1992 (R1997) (Permanence of Paper).

Library of Congress Cataloging-in-Publication Data

Names: Roche, David, 1976- author.
Title: Arrival / David Roche.
Other titles: 21st century film essentials.
Description: First edition. | Austin : University of Texas Press, 2024. | Series: 21st century film essentials | Includes bibliographical references and index.
Identifiers: LCCN 2024000577
ISBN 978-1-4773-3014-2 (hardcover)
ISBN 978-1-4773-3015-9 (paperback)
ISBN 978-1-4773-3016-6 (pdf)
ISBN 978-1-4773-3017-3 (epub)
Subjects: LCSH: Villeneuve, Denis, 1967—Criticism and interpretation. | Arrival (Motion picture : 2016) | Science fiction films—History and criticism. | LCGFT: Film criticism.
Classification: LCC PN1997.2.A674 R63 2024 | DDC 791.45/72—dc23/eng/20230224
LC record available at https://lccn.loc.gov/2024000577

doi:10.7560/330142

Contents

For my mom

ARRIVAL

Introduction

I first saw *Arrival* on its release in Toulouse with my friend and colleague Vincent Souladié after a long day of teaching. We stumbled out of the movie theater, basking in the emotions and sensations the movie experience had triggered, and stopped for a drink at Le Cardinal, a café on Place Wilson, hoping to maintain the feeling as long as possible. We agreed that we had probably just seen the greatest science fiction film since *Blade Runner* (Scott, 1982) and that, in many ways, *Arrival* had achieved what *Interstellar* (Nolan, 2014) had aimed for: hard science fiction that blends blockbuster spectacle with emotional and intellectual engagement. This book is an endeavor to put words to that first impression, which repeated viewings only enriched. It offers an in-depth analysis of the film's formal and thematic features and their aesthetic, political, and ethical implications, which, to someone like me who started out as a literary scholar, is a worthy enterprise. In proposing a book-length analysis, I am, in the close-reading tradition, simultaneously positing and attempting to prove the work's interest and potential contribution to the history of cinema and to our understanding of the medium.

I am not alone in finding the 2016 film worthy of interest. With an anti-war plot centered on an academic in the humanities who contributes to saving the world, *Arrival* is a humanities scholar's dream come true, and its proposal to take the humanities seriously is especially gratifying for those of us working in fields deemed not scientific and useful enough, and currently under threat from neoliberal policies. There are obviously more "objective" reasons for choosing to write a book on *Arrival*. The film makes for a highly interesting case study because, like most important works, it is both typical of certain trends and highly original.

For one, it is very much characteristic of the twenty-first-century Hollywood productions discussed by Geoff King in *Quality Hollywood: Markers of Distinction in Contemporary Studio Film*, published the year of *Arrival*'s release; the 2016 film is proof of the trend's continuance through the 2010s. In his book, King focuses on a group of Hollywood films—including *The Assassination of Jesse James by the Coward Robert Ford* (Dominik, 2007), *Inception* (Nolan, 2010), and *The Social Network* (Fincher, 2010)—that strive to strike a balance between qualities associated with the pejoratively connoted "mainstream" and the more "distinguished and valorized" independent sector.[1] King is well aware that Hollywood has always had a tradition of quality whose reasons and implications are very much historically determined (for instance, the wave of historical and literary movies of the 1920s as a means to counter attacks on Hollywood morality),[2] so he is mainly interested in assessing the late 2000s phenomenon's singularity and place in the history of Hollywood quality productions. King interrogates both how such films came to be in a post-Indiewood context marked by the "closure of a number of specialty divisions" and how they seek to present themselves as "better, more sophisticated, and more artistic" than the usual Hollywood fare, as "doing . . . particular *kinds* of things that have 'higher' associations"—in Bourdieusian terms, as holding a higher "cultural capital."[3] Characterized by qualities associated with both Hollywood cinema (action, spectacle, star power) and art and independent cinema ("dark, gloomy and sombre; subtle and nuanced; relatively complex; serious, sometimes perhaps morally ambiguous"), these films position themselves on the mainstream–art cinema spectrum to varying degrees in an effort to simultaneously establish the category of "mainstream art cinema" and present themselves as its exemplars.[4] King identifies numerous rhetorical markers of distinction in the paratexts (trailers, posters, interviews) and critical responses to the films, as well as within the films themselves; these markers include "literariness" (for instance, by adapting prestigious books and plays), auteurism, engagement with real-world issues, a critical (even pessimistic) attitude, in-depth characterization, lack of closure and happy endings, ambiguity, reflexivity, and, generally speaking, the sense that the film is addressing a knowing adult audience.[5] The present book will foreground how *Arrival*, like other contemporary films, lays claim to such distinctions of kind, mainly by analyzing the way it not only combines formal and thematic features associated with both mainstream blockbuster and art and independent cinemas, but plays them against each other, sometimes revealing unexpected points of convergence.

Analyzing a work that is at once paradigmatic and innovative may, as the writings of Roland Barthes repeatedly demonstrate, have the potential to open avenues onto more general and notably theoretical concerns. *Arrival* engages, more broadly, with many theoretical questions posed by film studies and raises philosophical questions touching on both temporality and ethics. Many of these aspects have received academic attention, with articles focusing on language and communication (Engle 2016, Chamberlain 2019, Nicol 2019), time (Fleming and Brown 2018, Mamula 2018, Sticchi 2018, Bréan 2021, Simon 2021, Gervais 2022), ethics (Krzych 2018, Sticchi 2018, Noletto and Lopes 2019, Zavota 2020), geopolitics (Fleming 2020), identity politics (Mayer 2017, Longfellow 2022), and reflexivity (Jaunas 2021). This book engages with these texts, exploring some of the more obvious lines of inquiry in a new light (language, communication, and metacommentary in chapter 3; time in chapter 4; politics and ethics in chapter 6), while paying attention to aspects that have gone largely ignored (adaptation and authorship in chapter 1, science fiction in chapter 2, space in chapter 5).

This book opens with a study of how the production mode, creative practices, and marketing and postmarketing strategies sought to discursively construct *Arrival* as an auteur adaptation positioned at the nexus of mainstream and art cinema. Chapter 2 then proposes to situate this particular alien invasion film generically, as a rare instance of a hard science fiction film that endeavors to debunk science fiction cinema conventions and value the humanities over the hard sciences. Chapter 3 pays attention to the film's reliance on linguistics and communication theories, not so much for the sake of verisimilitude but so as to make the humanities-based premise dramatically interesting; it then analyzes the film's quasi-historiographical metacommentary on film spectatorship and celebration of the omnicommunicativeness of an audiovisual medium. Chapters 4 and 5 focus on the film's explorations of time and space as thematic, narrative, dramatic, aesthetic, and philosophical stakes. Chapter 4 examines how *Arrival* exploits the dramatic potential of human beings' differing apprehensions of time, before delineating it as a mind-game film that seeks to express the subjectivity of the protagonist, Dr. Louise Banks, that demands repeated viewings, and that resists narrative closure because of the precariousness of its flashbacks/flash-forwards and its affinity with the crystalline regime of time-image cinema. Chapter 5 analyzes the narrative, dramatic, and symbolic functions of places before demonstrating how the film offers an exploration of sublime space without ever leaving Earth and attempts to evoke an alien time-space through its multiple reconfigurations of cinematic space. Finally, chapter 6 argues that the film favors ethics over politics, subordinating the genre's and contemporary blockbusters' compulsory geopolitical backdrop to the overall theme of communication, and calling on the woman's film as a framework with which to think through dilemmas associated with one's quest for the good life in light of a transcendent encounter with the Other.

Although this is a book whose main argument is that *Arrival* is, indeed, a highly important twenty-first-century film, it explores the borders of a series of relations—between mainstream and art cinema, hard and soft science fiction, time and space, politics and ethics—and is ultimately traversed by two main ideas: *Arrival* is about ethics and about cinema (it is a stellar example of meta), thereby raising the question of whether it is about the ethics of cinema. The analyses herein open up venues of inquiry that go far beyond the 2016 film itself. Does hard science fiction's interest in theory make it eminently discursive and thus literary? How relevant is the analogy between art and communication? What is cinematic space if not cinematic space-time? Does a film have the means to express an alien space-time and a hybrid human-alien subjectivity, or is the endeavor compromised by the limitations imposed by a production context, a medium, or even human knowledge and subjectivity? *Arrival*—the book on the film—does not provide definitive answers, but I hope that it offers insights into these questions.

Arrival as Auteur Film Adaptation

THE MAKING OF *ARRIVAL*

The story of *Arrival* is a love affair with a short story that provoked a chain reaction. It all started when Eric Heisserer, a screenwriter with a writer-director credit to his name for the 2013 film *Hours* and screenwriting credits for two horror remakes and one sequel (2010's *A Nightmare on Elm Street*, 2011's *Final Destination 5* and *The Thing*), discovered Ted Chiang's "Story of Your Life," first published in a 1998 issue of *Starlight* magazine and collected in the author's 2002 short story collection, *Stories of Your Life and Others*. Heisserer said he was so "emotionally affected" by the story that he became "obsessed" with it and wanted to "share it with more people."[1] If he admitted that the character of Louise Banks somewhat reminded him of his wife,[2] many other features of this hard science fiction story with a focus on language and communication may have resonated with the screenwriter; raised by a mother who would read science fiction to him on a regular basis and a father who, as a professor of ancient history, had a thing for learning foreign languages, Heisserer went on to work for an astrophysicist in Clear Lake City near NASA's

Johnson Space Center and enjoyed listening to fuddled scientists concoct elaborate theories at parties.[3] The screenwriter pitched the project to various producers and eventually sparked the interest of Dan Cohen, Dan Levine, and Shawn Levy of 21 Laps Entertainment,[4] who were surprised Chiang's story hadn't been optioned yet.[5] The producers then set out to look for a director.

Denis Villeneuve was by no means the obvious choice in 2013; though a big science fiction fan,[6] the Quebecois director was not the "science fiction master" that online commentators of *Dune: Part One* (2021) were to label him.[7] Although most audiences discovered him with his star-studded "US-American" films, *Prisoners* (2013), with Jake Gyllenhaal and Hugh Jackman, *Sicario* (2015), with Emily Blunt, Josh Brolin, and Benicio Del Toro, and especially *Arrival*, Villeneuve had already directed four feature films—*Un 32 août sur terre* (1998), *Maelström* (2000), *Polytechnique* (2009), and *Incendies* (2010)—as well as several shorts and one TV episode. His breakthrough French-language film, *Incendies*, had even represented Canada for Best Foreign Language Film at the 2011 Academy Awards and drawn the interest of Hollywood producers, who then approached him to direct *Prisoners*.[8]

Villeneuve expressed an immediate interest in 21 Laps Entertainment's "Story of Your Life" project, but he was working on *Prisoners* and had already committed to *Sicario*. He was also worried the story would be difficult to adapt.[9] For this reason, he proceeded to meet with Heisserer to discuss the project over coffee for a period of six months;[10] meanwhile, the writer labored on the screenplay while "pining" (his very words) for Villeneuve.[11] When the director finally committed to the project, he told Heisserer what he tells every screenwriter with whom he is about to embark on a project:

> I say two things. I'm going to be your best friend because I'll die trying to protect the poetry of your ideas, and sometimes I'm going to be your worst enemy because I'm going to do it my own. I will digest your words and create images with them and I'm going to be a traitor. I will stab you in the back. I will not respect, I will change things, and it will become my movie. I'm sorry.[12]

Having formulated this word of warning with what sounds like a mixture of honesty and self-derision, Villeneuve kept Heisserer on the team throughout production and invited him to see two edits during postproduction;[13] for a screenwriter used to meeting directors just to "pass on the baton,"[14] the collaboration was unlike anything Heisserer had experienced so far. Once committed, Villeneuve then reached out to actress Amy Adams, his first choice for the part of Louise Banks. The star was planning on taking a break after major roles in *American Hustle* (Russell, 2013) and *Big Eyes* (Burton, 2014), but she immediately fell in love with the project and accepted the part.[15] With a big star and an up-and-coming director secured, 21 Laps Entertainment could set the ball rolling, and by June 2015 Jeremy Renner, Forest Whitaker, and Michael Stuhlbarg had signed on as well.[16]

Many of Villeneuve's regular collaborators came on board: Icelandic composer Jóhann Jóhannsson, who had scored *Prisoners* and *Sicario*; British editor Joe Walker, who has cut all of Villeneuve's films since *Sicario*; US-American casting director

Francine Maisler, also on every Villeneuve project since *Sicario*; Quebecois production designer Patrice Vermette, a close collaborator since *Prisoners* and *Enemy* (2013); Canadian costume designer Renée April, who worked on all of Villeneuve's films from *Prisoners* to *Blade Runner 2049* (2017); and Canadian sound editor Sylvain Bellemare, an early collaborator of Villeneuve's who had worked on *Incendies* as well as on the feature film *Un 32 août sur la terre* and the television short *Next Floor* (2008). Visual effects (VFX) were subcontracted to, among others, Oblique FX, who had already worked on *Sicario*, and Rodeo FX and Framestore, who would later work on *Blade Runner 2049* and (in the case of Rodeo FX) *Dune* (2021). The core of the *Sicario* team was thus reunited, with the exception of established British cinematographer Roger Deakins, who was busy on another project and would return for *Blade Runner 2049* and *Dune*. To replace him, Villeneuve reached out to a talented young cinematographer, Bradford Young, whose work on *A Most Violent Year* (Chandor, 2014) he'd greatly admired.[17]

The making and marketing of *Arrival* are, in many ways, typical of many contemporary Hollywood productions: the idea did not originate with the director, but Villeneuve's practice and especially the production team's marketing and post-marketing discourses sought to position the director as the ultimate decision-maker, thereby branding the film an auteur film in the process. This strategy, identified by Thomas Elsaesser in a 1995 piece,[18] is manifest in the Blu-ray/DVD extras, each of which gives the director pride of place regardless of the area under discussion (linguistics, music, sound design, editing). The first, longest, and most prominent of the Sony Pictures Blu-ray extras, titled "Xenolinguistics: Understanding

Arrival,"[19] concludes with several comments that serve to establish the director's author-ity: production designer Patrice Vermette defines "Denis Villeneuve's signature" as an ability to get everybody "focused in the same direction"; producer Dan Levine then describes the "vibe on [Villeneuve's] set" as "from the top down," with a "brilliant" director who wants "feedback" and a cast and crew who "feel comfortable"; and the screenwriter rounds it off nicely with the clichéd view that Villeneuve is yet another artist who "exorcise[s] his demons" through his "dark," "intense," and "brutal" material—even if the latter did not originate with him in the first place. The postmarketing discourse characterizes Villeneuve the auteur as a gentle ruler, channeling the talents and ideas of others to express his vision and negotiate his own personal issues.

Villeneuve himself is quick to recognize the collaborative energies that fuel his films; he confesses that he dislikes working with people who "bring nothing" and feels that the "tension" created by the encounter between "strong artistic visions" creates "something stronger."[20] Also fairly typical of contemporary practices is his tendency to work with the same collaborators, a means of ensuring aesthetic cohesion and, more pragmatically, efficient teamwork once various relationships have been established—Villeneuve explains, for instance, that working with editor Joe Walker has become a "faster" and increasingly "familiar" process, and he concludes jokingly, "We don't need to be polite anymore."[21] Villeneuve's practice is thus similar to that of notable predecessors such as Steven Spielberg, David Fincher, and Christopher Nolan, who also work with the same composers, cinematographers, editors, production designers, and casting directors. More specific to the Denis Villeneuve team, perhaps, is that it is international in scope (albeit very much Western) while remaining firmly rooted in Villeneuve's homeland, an attitude toward Hollywood that recalls that of Mexican directors Alfonso Cuarón and Alejandro G. Iñárritu. In Villeneuve's case, perhaps, Canadian tax incentives might very well provide the perfect excuse for maintaining close ties to Quebec—and artistic license in the process—while profiting from Hollywood production and distribution.[22]

Thus labeled a Denis Villeneuve film, *Arrival* sheds some light on how the industry viewed film authorship in the late 2010s and how auteurism is currently being redefined and repackaged in relation to what C. Paul Sellors calls "collective authorship," in which the collective intentionality of the group and the individual intentions of its members are intermeshed to varying degrees.[23] Though the word is never uttered, auteurism is upheld as an aesthetic ideal—a "distinction," to use Geoff King's term—to be marketed and publicized, and it remains largely attached to the figure of the director. But the promotional discourses around *Arrival* also suggest that the idea of collective authorship—and notably the valuing of the input of actors, screenwriters, cinematographers, production designers, composers, sound designers, and so forth—has gained some currency in Hollywood by clearly identifying which members of the production team "count as members of the film's authorial body."[24] A Denis Villeneuve film is thus presented as a team effort led by the director, its visual style a synthesis of April's, Deakins's (or Young's in the case of *Arrival*), Vermette's, and the regular VFX teams' contributions. It is composed not only of "authored components," such as Johannssón's score or the heptapods' voices designed by Michelle Child and David Whitehead (both composers and sound designers are entitled to their own Blu-ray extras),[25] but also of "varying degrees of joint authorship,"[26] such as the hieroglyphs the production design team based on the screenwriter's idea of circles,[27] the cinematography that the cinematographer describes as a shared creative space ("We stood in the same room together and tried something"),[28] and, of course, the project's originating in Heisserer's love for Chiang's story. It is this picture of *collective auteurism*, I would suggest, that is simultaneously fashioned and promoted in the marketing and postmarketing material, and only an in-depth study of the production notes along with interviews of team members could possibly determine the degree of actual collaboration involved in the making of a film like *Arrival*.

Preproduction on *Arrival* started in January, with Vermette and his team designing the inside and base of the spacecraft.[29] Filming started on June 7, 2015, and lasted twelve weeks, according to editor Joe Walker.[30] The shoot was based in Montreal, with the university scenes shot at the University of Montreal, the Banks house scenes on nearby Île-Cadieux, and the Montana scenes near Saint-Fabien, roughly five hundred kilometers downstream at the mouth of the Saint Lawrence River. Villeneuve's dislike of VFX (he said he would have preferred to use animatronics)[31] led him to limit it to the scenes in which the actors interact with the white screen, which took two days to shoot.[32] Postproduction, a stage of the filmmaking process Villeneuve particularly enjoys,[33] lasted until June 2016.[34]

Arrival was presented at the Venice Film Festival on September 1, 2016, and the Toronto Film Festival on September 9; it was there that Heisserer, along with author Ted Chiang, watched the finished film for the first time. It then opened on November 10 in ten countries (Australia, Chile, Czechia, the UK, Hungary, and a few others) and on November 11 in seventeen more, including the United States and Canada. The film was both a box office and a critical success, earning $100 million in the United States and Canada and another $103 million worldwide. It performed well at the Venice Film Festival, winning the Arca CinemaGiovani (or Young Cinema) award. The film and screenplay also received awards from associations specializing in science fiction (Best Writing from the Academy of Science Fiction, Fantasy, and Horror Films; Outstanding Dramatic Presentation from Science Fiction and Fantasy Writers of America). *Arrival* was nominated for eight awards at the BAFTAS and the Academy Awards but won only technical ones (Best Sound in Great Britain and Sound Editing in the United States, for Sylvain Bellemare, Claude La Haye, and Bernard Gariéby Strobl). It was ranked number three on the *Guardian*'s list of best films of 2016.[35] *Arrival* has since received some academic attention (see the introduction), and Denis Villeneuve's importance in the contemporary filmscape has been recognized in academia with the publication of a collected volume in Edinburgh University Press's ReFocus series in January 2023.

ADAPTING "STORY OF YOUR LIFE"

Ted Chiang had only one collection of short stories to his name when Eric Heisserer discovered his work. A four-time recipient of both Nebula (1990, 1999, 2002, 2007) and Hugo (2002, 2008, 2009, 2011) Awards, he was mainly known in science fiction circles. And while the 2020 reedition of *Stories of Your Life and Others* boasts praise from Pulitzer Prize–winning authors Junot Díaz and Colson Whitehead alongside science fiction giant China Miéville and the prolific Joyce Carol Oates, the original 2002 edition published by Tor Books was accompanied by a blurb from an author known only to readers of science fiction, Greg Dale Bear. Clearly, adapting a Ted Chiang story did not come with the same economic guarantees as adapting J. K. Rowling, J. R. R. Tolkien, Stephen King, Philip K. Dick, or Neil Gaiman. In this case, it truly was the story that was being adapted, not the author, whose many awards, habitual markers of distinction, were not mentioned in the promotional material. The lack of a bankable name did come with one notable advantage that Alfred Hitchcock himself would have approved of: authorship need not be shared, unlike what Villeneuve would later experience with *Blade Runner 2049* and *Dune*.[36] The repeated mention of the story's power did, however, aim to assert the project's potential "literariness."

A sixty-two-page novella, "Story of Your Life" is narrated by Louise Banks, whose narratee, evoked in the title, is her daughter Hannah. The narrative alternates between two plotlines that receive (almost) equal attention: the story of Hannah's life and that of the heptapods' arrival, which is narrated in linear fashion. The story opens and closes on the moment when Louise and Ian decide to have a child; Hannah's "arrival," a word that is, significantly, used only in reference to her, thus frames the narrative.[37] The heptapod plot is related in classical fashion: it follows a linear trajectory and is narrated in the past tense. Hannah's life, however, is mostly narrated backward, from her death to her birth, in the present tense. Louise's post-heptapod relation to time seems to affect only her account of her daughter's life. Roughly ten pages into the story, she introduces a scene in which Hannah is a teenager as follows:

> I remember one day during the summer when you're sixteen. For once, the person waiting for her date to arrive is me. Of course, you'll be waiting around too, curious to see what he looks like. You'll have a friend of yours, a blond girl, with the unlikely name of Roxie, hanging out with you, giggling.
>
> "You may feel the urge to make comments about him," I'll say, checking myself in the hallway mirror. "Just restrain yourselves until we leave."[38]

The text flouts common usage of tense and aspect: the opening verbal syntagma begs for a past tense whose possibility the contraction renders unlikely, since it is more commonly used with the present tense; the modal "will" is deflected from indicating a "prediction" or "volition" to evoking a future that is as definite as the past;[39] the use of "-ing" as the marker of an event that is "not necessarily complete" sets the scene in medias res, thereby reinforcing the sense that Louise is experiencing the events she is describing as she narrates.[40] This complex use of tense and aspect, which is repeated in later scenes,[41] makes it difficult to pinpoint narrating time (the time Louise the narrator is actually speaking from): Is she seeing the future? Has she already experienced it? In other words, is it actually past? Or are past and future paradoxically one and the same once you have achieved a heptapod worldview?

Adapting a story that relies so much on the possibilities of language as a medium was going to be no easy feat indeed, as Villeneuve pointed out to Heisserer, but the challenge itself can be seen as yet another marker of distinction. The screenwriter, producers, and director all insisted on their common ambition to reproduce the emotion they experienced while reading the story.

> HEISSERER: When I hit "Story of Your Life," I had to put [the book] down because I was so emotionally affected [. . .] I wanted to, like, lift the feeling that I got and put it into a movie.[42]

> LEVINE: The movie is filled with ideas, as was the story, but it's also profoundly emotional.[43]

> VILLENEUVE: I was hoping [. . .] that [the film] would convey the emotion that I felt when I was reading the short story, and I fought to protect those emotions throughout the process.[44]

These statements of intent tend to confirm Colin MacCabe's claim that, while adaptation studies have derided the criterion of fidelity, it remains a central idea(l) for both filmmakers and audiences.[45] What emerges from Heisserer's, Levine's, and Villeneuve's comments, however, has less to do with fidelity to the text itself than with making a film that is, in MacCabe's words, "true to the spirit" of the text, its emotions and ideas.[46] The adapters clearly believed that a faithful adaptation might require major modifications and thus constitute a process not dissimilar to that of turning a screenplay into a film. Villeneuve's words of warning to his screenwriters—that respecting the "poetry" of a text implies "digesting . . . words and creating images with them," thereby betraying the source—equally apply to the *Arrival* production team's shared view of film adaptation.

Although Villeneuve initially expressed doubt about the story's adaptability, he admitted that he was "impressed" with Heisserer's screenplay,[47] which had led the writer "to go far away from the short story" in order to find a "dramatic structure in a short story that was very difficult to adapt."[48] Heisserer himself was very much aware that making the story "cinematic" was going to be quite a challenge:

> My prime directive was to take the way the short story made me feel and kind of gently lift that from the source material and find a way to transplant that into a film because I was just emotionally affected by the short so much. I found later that the biggest challenge was really how to make it cinematic because Ted's story works so well as a piece of literary fiction, but it didn't need conflict the way that a movie does. And so the first big change that I had to make was in the way that the aliens communicate with us. In the story, they deliver basically intergalactic TV screens and we have a very long expensive Skype call with them. And it goes for about a year really of just back and forth—or a prolonged period of time. And that made for a very flat narrative for film. The big change that I made early on that had a giant ripple effect and sort of set me on a course from then on was for them to show up at our front door, and have it be a face-to-face meeting. As a first contact story, it created a lot of tension and a lot of geopolitical panic that allowed the tension to escalate throughout the film.[49]

Interestingly enough, what the screenwriter calls "cinematic" has little to do with images and sounds, and would better be described as "dramatic." Instead of discussing the difficulty of adapting a first-person narrative about language in an audiovisual medium, Heisserer insists on the necessity of altering elements involving time (a reduced time-setting), space ("our front door," "geopolitical"), and action ("conflict," "panic," "tension") that basically correspond to the classical unities of tragedy. Making the story "cinematic," in Heisserer's mind, implicitly entailed fashioning it into the canonical story form typical of classical narration (David Bordwell's discussion of classical narration very much relies on the three unities) and introducing a dramatic tension that could build up to a climax.[50] It also entailed introducing a modicum of the "face-to-face" encounter of the alien invasion narrative Chiang had so deliberately and deftly avoided. On first glance, then, capturing the spirit of Chiang's story meant trapping it within the codified generic narrative and dramatic structures of Hollywood cinema, paradoxically downplaying elements that granted it literary distinction.

The major changes brought to the story are as follows: the time-setting of the heptapod plot is reduced to a period of twenty-eight days; the mode of communication is altered; the film focuses entirely on the hieroglyphs (Heptapod B in Chiang's story) and ignores the analysis of oral language (Heptapod A); Hannah does not die in a rock-climbing accident as a young adult but from cancer at the age of twelve; the film's "narrator" (Louise in voice-over) is restricted to the opening and closing scenes; the story's alternating story levels (moving forward with the heptapod story and mostly backward with Hannah's life) are replaced by a flash-forward structure that frames the mostly linear narrative of the heptapods' arrival (Heisserer explains that he came up with the flash-forward structure early on and that the Hannah scenes accompanied by Louise's voice-over underwent very few revisions).[51] Though Villeneuve repeatedly insisted on how impressed he was with Heisserer's work, he added that "together [they] went back to the themes and some things that [Villeneuve] love[d] in the short story, so slowly [they] travelled towards it with this beautiful structure."[52] Further adjustments were made during production and postproduction[53] (both the popular-science documentary and Louise's nightmare sequences were, apparently, conceived in the editing room[54]).

Today, *Arrival* appears as the film that launched Villeneuve's science fiction blockbuster cycle, confirmed the composition of his international albeit Canadian-based team, consolidated collective auteurism as a Denis Villeneuve brand and practice, and gave the director economic clout in Hollywood, as well as critical and academic stature among audiences. Villeneuve's career would confirm Geoff King's observation that "stability and success [whether critical or at the box office] in Hollywood can also be precisely what creates space for innovation."[55] Villeneuve is comparable, in this respect, to Christopher Nolan, whose position in Hollywood, following the success of *The Dark Knight* (2008), gave him enough leverage and "artistic freedom" to make a blockbuster puzzle movie like *Inception* (2011).[56] Unlike Nolan, however, Villeneuve was less involved in screenwriting from *Prisoners* to *Blade Runner 2049* (though he has taken up the pen again for both installments of *Dune*). *Arrival* is the work of many adapters, chiefly the screenwriter and director, who endeavored to be faithful to the spirit of Chiang's story, to its ideas and, more subjectively, to its emotions rather than to its linguistic intricacies. Collective authorship should clearly be expanded to include the writer as well, who is also often mentioned in interviews and himself interviewed in the postmarketing material proposed on the Blu-ray/DVD release. Clearly, the collective intention was to make a film that had clear markers of distinction (an Oscar-contender director, a complex literary source) but that would be neither too artsy nor too serious—more like Heisserer's favorite science fiction film, *Close Encounters of the Third Kind* (Spielberg, 1977) than, say, *2001: A Space Odyssey* (Kubrick, 1968) or *Solaris* (Tarkovsky, 1972).[57] In what follows, we will see to what extent *Arrival* is formally and thematically inhabited by a tension between classical forms (genre, narration) and more "poetic" ones that might do justice, so to speak, to Chiang's poetry without being its audiovisual equivalent.[58]

Arrival as Hard Soft Science Fiction

TRADITIONS IN SCIENCE FICTION FILM

Arrival is at once characteristic of a contemporary trend in quality Hollywood science fiction films, exemplary of a popular science fiction subgenre (the alien invasion movie), and yet highly exceptional as a hard science fiction film about linguistics. The 2016 film is part of a cycle of productions—including *Inception*, *Gravity* (Cuarón, 2013), *Interstellar*, and *The Martian* (Scott, 2015)—whose stated ambitions are to fulfill the legacy of Hollywood productions like *2001*, *Slaughterhouse-Five* (Hill, 1972), and *Blade Runner* (Scott, 1982) by attempting to bridge the boundaries between art and mainstream cinema. Ridley Scott and Christopher Nolan figure prominently in this respect: Scott as a peer and director of benchmark genre films such as *Alien* (1979) and *Blade Runner* that have had a lasting influence on sci-fi horror and dystopian films and series, Nolan as the current cycle's initiator and (until recently) frontrunner. Villeneuve has been open about his admiration for both artists; he admitted that he "had the responsibility to respect and honor" Scott's 1982 masterpiece when working on its 2017 sequel,[1] and he described himself as "the biggest Christopher Nolan fan in the world," called the British director a "Master,"[2] and professed an appreciation for the breadth of his scope,[3] even for the less financially and critically successful *Tenet* (2020).[4] The esteem is reciprocal, with Nolan describing *Dune: Part One* (2021) as a "gift for film fans."[5] The two directors consolidated their artistic kinship by doing a Q&A at Los Angeles's DGA theater in November 2021 in the wake of *Dune: Part One*'s release, in which Nolan questioned Villeneuve about the film's artistic choices.[6] Fans and the media have noted the similarities between the two directors, one magazine article title going so far as to raise the question "Is Denis Villeneuve the New Christopher Nolan?"[7] The back-to-back releases of *Arrival*, *Blade Runner 2049*, *Dune: Part One*, and *Dune: Part Two* (2024) have indeed positioned Villeneuve as the new main player in the field.

Arrival is somewhat of an exception to the abovementioned cycle because its $47 million budget is not high enough for it to qualify as a blockbuster by twenty-first-century Hollywood standards. Compare it to $90 million for *Ad Astra*, $100 million for *Gravity*, $108 million for *The Martian*, $150 million for *Blade Runner 2049*, $160 million for *Inception*, and $165 million for both *Dune: Part One* and *Interstellar*. However, it remains a more comfortable budget than those of independent productions like *Moon* (Jones, 2009) and *High Life* (Denis, 2018), produced for $5 million and $8 million, respectively, or even *Midnight Special* (Nichols, 2016), made for $18 million. *Arrival* also made less (roughly $203 million worldwide) than *Inception*, *Gravity*, *Interstellar*, or *The Martian*, which all made over $600 million, but it grossed almost as much as *Blade Runner 2049*, which underperformed (at $259 million). *Arrival*'s ambitions and treatment of its material are nonetheless very similar to those of *Gravity*, *Interstellar*, and *The Martian*: a global issue is considered from an individual perspective (environmental issues in *Interstellar* and *The Martian*), requiring a reduced cast of characters; the protagonist is a scientist torn between their mission and status as a parent (*Gravity*, *Interstellar*); alien invasion and/or space opera spectacle coexist alongside more intimate stakes that have psychological, moral, and philosophical implications à la *2001* and *Solaris*, or more recently *Close Encounters of the Third Kind* and *Signs* (Shyamalan, 2002) (*Gravity*, *Interstellar*, *The Martian*). Everything is geared to bridge the gap between popular and art cinema, bringing to mind Villeneuve's praise-filled words when describing Nolan's films' main achievement: "To bring intellectual concepts and to bring them in that scope to the screen."[8] The French Canadian director, as Brenda Longfellow notes, has clearly retained his "art film sensibility,"[9] which he vocally promotes in order to align his work with that of his peers and distinguish it from the mainstream. In 2018 Villeneuve stated his intentions regarding the *Dune* project thus: "The ambition is to make the Star Wars movie I never saw. In a way, it's Star Wars for adults."[10]

Arrival revisits a genre—the alien invasion movie—that was particularly popular in the 1950s in both the United States and United Kingdom. Resonating with the Cold War context,[11] the aliens often metaphorically embody the destructive forces of totalitarianism (the 1951 *The Man from Planet X* and *The Thing from Another World*; the 1953 *Invaders from Mars*, *The Quatermass Xperiment*, and *The War of the Worlds*; and their remakes, sequels, and spawns, including the 1955 *The Quatermass Xperiment*, the 1956 *Earth vs. the Flying Saucers*, and the 1957 *Invasion of the Saucer-Men* and *The Brain from Planet*

Arous), sometimes already living in our midst (the 1956 *Invasion of the Body Snatchers*, the 1960 *Village of the Damned*, and the 1967–1968 ABC series *The Invaders*), or, far more exceptionally, despairing of humanity's inability to live in peace and harmony (the 1951 *The Day the Earth Stood Still*). Having run out of steam by the late 1960s, the subgenre was resurrected by Steven Spielberg on several occasions, as director (the 1977 *Close Encounters of the Third Kind*, the 1982 *E.T.*, and the 2005 *War of the Worlds*), and producer (the *Men in Black* franchise, launched in 1997, and the 2011 *Super 8*), sparking renewed interest in the genre in both cinema (the 1978 *Invasion of the Body Snatchers*, the 1982 *The Thing*, the 1987 *The Hidden*, the 1988 *They Live*, the 1996 *Independence Day* and *Mars Attacks!*, the 2002 *Signs*) and television (*V* 1983–1985, *War of the Worlds* 1988–1990, *The X-Files* 1993–2018). Alien invasion movies all have the same basic premise, as the subgenre's name indicates; it is the treatment that can differ from one work to another, often through combination with other genres, modes, and narratives—from disaster movie (*War of the Worlds*), horror (*The Thing*, *The Hidden*), and comedy (*Men in Black*) to moral fable (*The Day the Earth Stood Still*), jingoistic fare (*Independence Day*), political allegory (the 1956 *Invasion of the Body Snatchers*), satire (*They Live*, *Mars Attacks!*), and initiation story (*Close Encounters of the Third Kind*, *E.T.*).

The premise of *Arrival* is by no means exceptional, and it is hardly surprising that Heisserer's solution for making the story more cinematic was to imitate his favorite science fiction film, *Close Encounters of the Third Kind*, by having the aliens "show up at our front door." The title and several of the posters depicting helicopters and battleships surrounding a UFO suggest that the film will explore familiar territory (the military response to an alien landing) and that its primary novelty as far as the subgenre is concerned will be to focus exclusively on a specific stage of the alien invasion narrative, one that is usually limited to the role of inciting event (*The Day the Earth Stood Still*, *The Man from Planet X*, *The War of the Worlds*, *E.T.*, *V*, *Independence Day*, *Mars Attacks!*, etc.), with an occasional buildup to a climax (*Earth vs. the Flying Saucers*, *Close Encounters of the Third Kind*). *Arrival* proposes to take the problem posed by the alien invasion premise seriously: given how difficult it is just to communicate with humans in a hitherto unknown language, how would we even communicate with an alien life-form? The attempt to imagine an answer to this question situates both the film and the story it is based on in the realm of hard science fiction.

The term "hard science fiction" was coined in 1957 by P. Schuyler Miller, a book reviewer for the sci-fi magazine *Astounding*, to describe a body of works based on scientific principles that predominantly emerged in the 1950s.[12] It was defined by writer Allen Steele in a 1992 magazine article as "the form of imaginative literature that uses either established or carefully extrapolated science as its backbone,"[13] and later by science fiction scholar Gary Westfahl as "a form of science fiction that displays an especially heightened concern for, and an especially heightened connection to, science," with main features including "thorough explanations of scientific facts and/or lengthy expository passages providing evidence of a scientific thought process at work."[14] Westfahl notes that hard science fiction has often been understood as necessarily equated to an interest in hard science and objects, thus excluding writers, like Ursula K. Le Guin and Chad Oliver, who "bring to their writing a background in anthropology that makes their extrapolated aliens and future societies every bit as fascinating and intellectually involving as the technological marvels and strange planets of hard science fiction."[15] So a linguistics-centered alien invasion movie would not necessarily be an obvious hard science fiction candidate.

An important trend in literature (Arthur C. Clarke, Hal Clement, Robert A. Heinlein, Larry Niven, Kobo Abe, Stanisław Lem, Arkady and Boris Strugatsky, Octavia Butler, and Greg Bear feature among the classic authors, Ted Chiang and Liu Cixin among some of the notable twenty-first-century ones), hard science fiction has never held pride of place in film history. Of the works regularly cited in some of the hard science fiction film lists posted on popular websites (*Destination Moon*, 1959; *2001*; *Marooned*, 1969; *THX 1138*, 1971; *Silent Running*, 1972; *Blade Runner*; *Abyss*, 1989; *Contact*, 1997; *Gattaca*, 1997; *Sunshine*, 2007),[16] most would not remotely qualify as hard science fiction if set in comparison to hard science fiction novels or stories. The "hardest" of these science fiction films would probably include *Destination Moon* (and its spawn, the 1953 *Project Moonbase*, also based on a script by Heinlein, the 1954 *Riders to the Stars*, and the 1955 *Conquest of Space*),[17] *2001*, *Marooned*, *The Andromeda Strain*, and *Contact*, significantly all based on the works of, or written for the screen by, science fiction writers at least partly associated with hard science fiction (Heinlein, Clarke, Martin Caidin, and Michael Crichton, respectively) and astronomy (Carl Sagan). In most films, astrophysics, biology, and other fields offer neat premises, but it is the practical and moral consequences of various experiments, discoveries, and theories, more than their actual processes and theoretical implications, that are deemed worthy of interest and thus of dramatization. These consequences can present spectacular life-or-death situations that require immediate responses and hopefully solutions, or more ambiguous moral and political problems that threaten to compromise humanity. Though the protagonists are often scientists, the narrative speedily enters the realm of the action movie, often via other genres—the disaster movie in *Destination Moon*, *Marooned*, *Gravity*, and *The Martian*; noir in *Outland* (1981) and *Blade Runner*; horror in *Sunshine* and *Annihilation* (2018)—rather than taking the time to foreground their activities as they work through a problem. This may explain why science fiction cinema has largely been dominated not only by the alien invasion movie but by sci-fi horror in which horror takes over a science fiction premise (*The Quatermass Experiment* films, *The Thing*, *Invasion of the Body Snatchers*, *Alien*, *Sunshine*, *Annihilation*), the space opera in which adventure gets the upper hand (*Star Trek*, *Star Wars*, the 1978–1979 *Battlestar Galactica* and its remake), and dystopia, which explores the social and political problems of a future society (*Metropolis*, 1927; *Alphaville*, 1965; *Fahrenheit 451*, 1966; *Soylent Green*, 1973; *Logan's Run*, 1976; *Blade Runner*; *Nineteen Eighty-Four*, 1985; *Gattaca*; *Minority Report*, 2002; *Her*, 2013; *The Handmaid's Tale*, 2017). The focus on scientists as protagonists is certainly not enough for a given work to qualify as hard science fiction. Hard science fiction, cinema seems to prove, is not so much a genre or a "subgenre" as an attitude to the material that puts emphasis on science because it is deemed intellectually and imaginatively compelling.[18]

In Heisserer's and Villeneuve's cases at least, the appeal of hard science fiction seems to go hand in hand with a general interest in science. Relating a moviegoing experience with a group of rocket scientists who were horrified at *Armageddon*'s

(1998) representation of NASA personnel, Heisserer remembered thinking, "If I ever represent people like this in a movie, I gotta make sure they don't get up and leave the theater."[19] Villeneuve's own interest is, perhaps, traceable to when he studied science at a CÉGEP (Collège d'Enseignement Général Et Professionnel) before moving on to cinema at the Université du Québec in Montréal;[20] his taste for hard science fiction is certainly confirmed by his interest in adapting Arthur C. Clarke's 1973 novel *Rendezvous with Rama*.[21] For *Arrival*, Villeneuve and production designer Patrice Vermette not only drew on scientific imagery as a source of inspiration—the Shells were modeled on an asteroid named 15 Eunomia, the heptapods on deep-sea squid[22]—but endeavored to get some of the science right by using real software (Mathematica) to analyze the heptapods' language and employing, like the Nolan brothers for *Interstellar*,[23] scientists as consultants (in this case, Mayan-language expert Jessica Coon and computer experts Stephen and Christopher Wolfram).[24] Aesthetic and marketing interests herein converge, since advertising departments can then market a film's scientific credentials in its promotional material (Stephen Wolfram is featured on one of the Blu-ray extras).[25] Hard science fiction has value; sometimes presented as "the most rigorous and intellectually demanding form of science fiction," it is often celebrated at the expense of other forms of science fiction, "implying that those who do not produce it are somehow failing to realize the true potential of science fiction."[26] In this respect, hard science fiction's claim to distinction overlaps that of art cinema. Thematically at least, the recourse to hard science fiction is instrumental in framing films like *Interstellar* and *Arrival* as being not mindless action blockbusters but mainstream art cinema (my Netflix account, amusingly, includes them in the category "Intellectual Science Fiction"). The "hardness" of *Inception*, *Gravity*, *Interstellar*, *The Martian*, and *Arrival* qualifies the promise of blockbuster special-effect-based spectacle by modifying its nature: the spectacle will not be so much dispelled as grounded in serious scientific ideas and practices, even if the latter have since been disproven, as is the case with the Sapir-Whorf hypothesis *Arrival* draws on.[27]

If hard science fiction is an attitude, then any science fiction subgenre can be approached from a hard science fiction perspective. This is what *Arrival* proposes to do with the alien invasion subgenre. The 2016 film's predecessor in this and many other respects is *Contact* (directed by Robert Zemeckis), a debt acknowledged by *Arrival*'s alternative titles (*Contact* and *First Contact*) used in the Republic of Korea, France, and Portugal. *Contact* was released a year before the publication of Chiang's short story, so it is by no means certain that the story was influenced by the film, but Sagan's 1985 novel may very well have been a source of inspiration. The similarities are manifold. *Contact* is the story of scientists who decipher radio transmissions coming from space detailing the blueprint of a mysterious machine. The two films feature female leads, and it is the aliens' intentions, and thus the nature of their message, that constitute the main source of interest. In *Contact*, this is soon resolved, as the aliens utilize math like humans and Eleanor Arroway's (Jodie Foster) secret benefactor, S. R. Hadden (John Hurt), miraculously unravels the 3D logic of the documents they are sending. *Contact* is, however, typical of most hard science fiction cinema insofar as it never really explores how these problems are resolved, and ultimately the film's main thrust involves the tension between scientific and religious worldviews as embodied by Eleanor Arroway and Reverend Palmer Joss (Matthew McConaughey).

In the majority of alien invasion films, the science of communication is of little interest because it gets in the way of the motives needed to launch a causal-based, action-driven genre narrative—or it is believed to do so, at least. The problem is thus circumvented. Language is generally transparent;[28] the aliens' superior intelligence often enables them to speak or learn English (*The Day the Earth Stood Still*, *E.T.*, *V*), devise handy automatic translation machines (*Earth vs. the Flying Saucers*, the 1980s series *The War of the Worlds*, *Mars Attacks!*), or respond to a "universal language" such as math (*The Man from Planet X*, *Contact*) or music (*Close Encounters of the Third Kind*); and utter lack of communication is usually a sure sign of immediate threat (*War of the Worlds*, *The Thing*, *Alien*).[29] In "Story of Your Life," Louise, the voice of science, debunks the narrative shortcut-turned-cliché the vast majority of alien invasion stories rely on when Colonel Weber deduces from her reaction the following: "You seem to be implying that no alien could have learned human languages by monitoring our broadcasts."[30] Like Chiang's story, *Arrival* proposes to consider the possibility that the aliens' language, bodies, and cognition might, in effect, be so alien that teaching our language or learning theirs would be mission impossible. It is this impossible mission the film proposes to dramatize.

PLAYING WITH GENRE CONVENTIONS

Both "Story of Your Life" and *Arrival* recycle a host of science fiction tropes. In the story, the heptapods admit they came to "observe" humanity,[31] humans and aliens exchange gifts,[32] and some genre tropes are even playfully displaced through language (the "three tripod-mounted video cameras," for instance, recall the alien culture of *War of the Worlds*, in which everything comes in threes, so that what is a profoundly alien characteristic in one work is a human one in another[33]). *Arrival*'s UFO and alien design exploit familiar science fiction cinema imagery. Regardless of Villeneuve's stated intentions, the Shells hovering motionless on an axis perpendicular to Earth inevitably bring to mind the monoliths from *2001* while the ominous cloudbank spilling over the nearby mountains recalls the storms the flying saucers emerge from in *Close Encounters of the Third Kind* and *Independence Day*.[34] The heptapods resemble Cephalopoda and thus organisms endemic to Earth, like other film aliens who appear as humanoid (*The Day the Earth Stood Still*, *The Man from Planet X*, *Earth vs. the Flying Saucers*, *Close Encounters of the Third Kind*, *The X-Files*), reptilian (the *Alien* franchise, *V*), or insectoid (*Starship Troopers*, *Pitch Black*). The heptapod design intentionally reprises sci-fi horror imagery indebted to the giant bug/fish of the 1950s (particularly the radioactive octopus from the 1955 *It Came from Beneath the Sea*) and (like *Alien*) to Lovecraft.[35] The heptapods resemble monumental versions of *Galaxy Quest*'s (1999) octopodan Thermians and *Doctor Who*'s (BBC, 2005–) Daleks. They are, besides, a patchwork of science fiction references: their tentacles recall those of the xenomorphs from the *Alien* franchise, their globulous heads the 1957 *The Brain from Planet Arous* and the Martians of *Mars Attacks!*; the singular number of digits (in this case, seven) recalls the Martians from *The War of the Worlds*, their language "the 'telegraphic-schizophrenic' methods of the Tralfamadorians in [Kurt] Vonnegut's [1969 novel] *Slaughterhouse 5*."[36]

Following the prologue, the scene that sets up the basic premise, with a representative of the military soliciting the help of a scientist, is modeled on many classic scenes of the genre (*The Quatermass Experiment*) and turns out to be intensely aware of the many tropes it is revisiting. Upon introducing himself to Louise Banks, Colonel Weber speedily formulates her potential mission ("There's something I need you to translate for me") and, without allowing time for her to utter a quite unnecessary "What?," plays a recording for her. On it, a male voice can be heard asking, "Why are you here?"; it is followed by a low guttural sound that is presumably an alien speaking. The male voice then asks, "Where did you come from?," and Weber switches off the device and tells Louise, "Now you had it. What do you make of it?" The technological mediation is a dramatic device meant to delay the revelation of the heptapods' physical appearance, as Vincent Jaunas has noted;[37] it also reflexively foregrounds the familiarity of the premise, harking back to the legacy of a famous audio dramatization of the same generic premise: the Mercury Theater's October 30, 1938, radio performance of *The War of the Worlds*. The scene as a whole captures the absurdity of any alien encounter narrative. Following the insertion of the digital recorder, a medium close-up remains focused on Louise, registering her reaction for fourteen seconds: she is listening, but she is also looking down at the recording device (figs. 2.1.1–2.1.2). The direction of her gaze is meant to express her attention, of course, but it also makes sense in relation to the device itself, whose screen just relayed the faint decibel level of the human voices; the levels of the heptapods' blaring voices are, significantly, relegated offscreen. At this stage, Louise is constructed as a surrogate audience member, and we are invited to share her discovery of what the military have already heard and puzzled over; Louise is herself the object of Weber's attention, who is shown studying her in a medium shot (fig. 2.1.3), foreshadowing the many times Weber will observe the scientists at work in Montana. Dr. Banks, the linguist, is thus confronted with the absurdity of the habitual treatment of the alien invasion narrative, at least as it has been exploited by popular media. As in Chiang's story, it is indirectly through her response, witnessed by Weber, that the alien invasion cliché is debunked. Her profession as a scientist does not allow her to offer the "quick" translation Weber desires—the shadows on the right side of her face produced by the backlighting certainly emphasize that she is very much in the dark. All Louise can offer by way of answer are questions ("How many speaking?" "Do they have mouths?") and a methodology that does not suit the military and political need for speed and secrecy ("I can tell you it's impossible to translate from an audio file. I would need to be there—to interact with them"). Her reaction is thus the formulation of the film's serious approach to its hackneyed material and an invitation for us to recognize the absurdity of the clichés as such: who on earth could possibly translate these sounds as fast as they would for a human language such as Farsi? Louise's proposition sets up an alternative path for the alien invasion narrative that will be taken up in spite of Weber's initial refusal, conferring upon the film as a whole a seriousness that will be regularly set against the genre tropes the film identifies as clichés.

For the alien invasion clichés never entirely go away; on the contrary, they constitute the narrative's backbone. They circulate mainly via two of the three main actors of the alien invasion movie already present in the model of the genre, *The*

Figures 2.1.1–2.1.3. Louise listens to Weber's recording, on which a man asks the heptapods what their purpose is. She can offer only questions, not answers, drawing attention to the absurdity of this staple alien invasion narrative scene.

War of the Worlds: the media and the military (the scientists compose the third group). The familiarity of these tropes, which Sontag had in 1965 already identified as constituting "phase" 3 in a "model" science fiction scenario,[38] is such that the voices and sounds coming from the television Louise turns on in class are enough to inform both the diegetic and actual audiences that we are facing a *War of the Worlds*–like situation, the narration focusing on Louise's face in medium close-up and the television screen only appearing later in the left background of the very long shot of the auditorium that concludes the sequence (figs. 2.2.1–2.2.2). The soundtrack keeps playing the news coming from the radio or television as Louise returns home, and it ends with one reporter wondering, "If this is some sort of peaceful first contact, why send twelve? Why not just one?"—the line reflexively referring to both the subgenre and maybe even *Contact*. The "breaking news" the media in such movies is meant to bring is so familiar that it can easily be relegated to the visual background (Louise's TV in her bedroom or laptop in her office) or aural backdrop (when she returns home). The audiovisual media images recur at transitional moments in montage sequences that are the twenty-first-century globalization updates of the news report sequences present in films such as *When Worlds Collide* and *Earth vs. the Flying Saucers*.[39] The sounds and images, familiar from both film genre and media coverage of natural catastrophes and armed conflicts, provide grounding when the main plot appears to be lagging. They often serve the purpose of accumulation, the screens proposing not so much essential information for the characters and viewers as a bevy of media and genre clichés. These sequences thus fulfill a two-pronged function that is both contradictory and

Figures 2.2.1–2.2.2. The media images of the arrival disrupt Dr. Banks's class and immediately become a highly familiar visual and aural backdrop.

complementary: injecting familiarity, momentum, and drama while stimulating interest in the more novel, intimate hard science approach offered by the main plot.

Indeed, the military presence so essential to the alien invasion movie frames the revisited premise in every respect: in terms of narrative (they have missioned the scientists), space (the base and the military personnel), and time (the military, with the government behind it, repeatedly tries to impose its deadlines). The military is especially present on the soundtrack, which is regularly inhabited by staple science fiction dialogue and sounds. On their first visit inside the Shell, Louise, Ian, Colonel Weber, and the other men are accompanied by a mostly indistinct radio babble, much like astronauts working in space conversing with ground control in films like *Destination Moon*, *2001*, *Marooned*, *Apollo 13* (1995), and *Gravity*. Even equipped with quality headphones, all we can really distinguish are phrases like "Copy, Condor. Beginning our ascent now," "Oxygen level: 20.3 percent," "Gravity: .97," and "Team is in position," just barely piercing through the beeps and static noise (this is already the case in the helicopter, where the word "contact" can be made out in spite of the rotors' drone). The jargon and numbers operate more as signs of astronomy and the military than as data we are meant to puzzle over and ultimately comprehend; they signify as markers of science fiction and the cinematic military—language unfamiliar to most of us in the real world is nonetheless eminently familiar to us in similar situations depicted in war and science fiction movies.

The military backdrop nonetheless threatens to boil over halfway through the film. As far as genre is concerned, the bombing of the Shell works as a subplot that counters the hard science line imposed by Louise, Ian, and her team (and the makers of *Arrival*, of course) and seeks to steer the film back to the familiar territory of the *War of the Worlds* narrative, one that presupposes that the aliens' intentions are hostile and that immediate action is required. Significantly, it coalesces when the linguistic premise appears to be lagging. Though its source may differ, the sense of frustration experienced by the instigators within the diegesis potentially mirrors that of actual audiences bored with the linguistics-based plot. A pair of taciturn soldiers are first shown silently watching the scientists (figs. 2.3.1–2.3.2); one of them is Captain Marks, the camera operator, who, like us, has been observing the scientists at work from up close. The news that reaches the soldiers from the outside world is yet another bundle of sci-fi horror clichés: Marks's panicked partner tells him that their daughter is worried "the monsters are going to kill daddy," while social media personalities like the speaker on the post "Aliens Invade: Government Asleep at the Wheel" seek to sow political distrust: "Look at these people. Most of them don't even have guns. We could be facing a full-scale invasion and our president is just willing to sit back and let them waltz in and take our country" (fig. 2.3.3). On the meta level, the comment suggests that a majority of the audience may very well be "falling asleep" in front of a hard science fiction film whose filmmakers might have overlooked impatience as a possible response.

The bombing scene functions as an attempt to inject some staple sci-fi action blockbuster sound and imagery into a film that may, for some viewers, be deemed critically lacking in that department. Because the subplot is so familiar, it can be narrated elliptically (a characteristic of Villeneuve's narrative style, especially in *Prisoners*), with three thirty-seconds-long scenes leading to a very short enactment, which is equally brief (fifty seconds), silent (the men don't speak, and Marks refuses to answer Condor when the latter asks him what they're up to), and elliptical (the three sequences comprise ten shots in all). The bomb, whose timer is set at ten minutes, instills a sense of urgency, dramatically redoubling the more global urgency following General Shang's decision to cut transmissions, which constitutes a direct call for such action (military action within the diegesis, drama and spectacle from narrative and aesthetic perspectives). Ironically, while Weber and his team, seated in

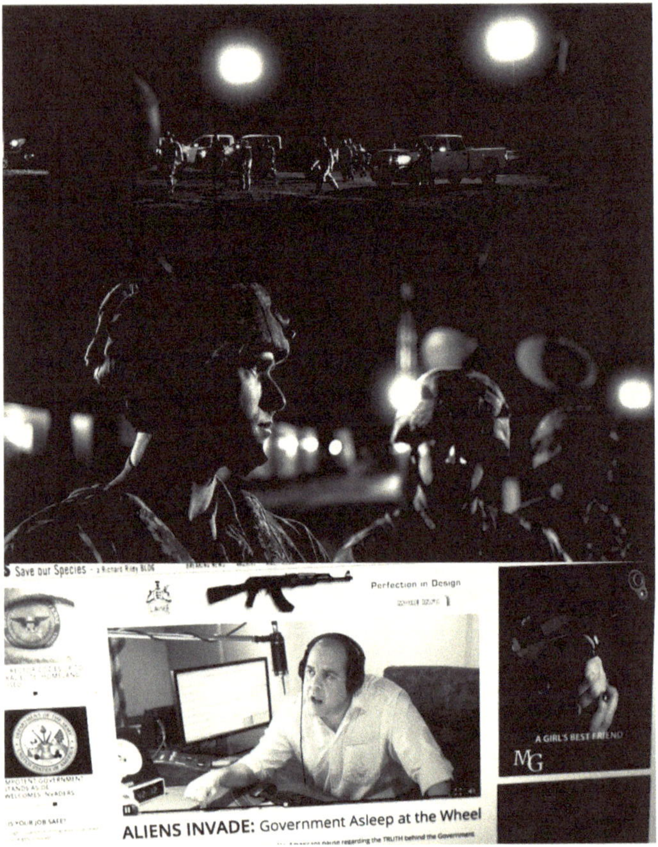

Figures 2.3.1–2.3.3. Captain Marks, who has been watching the scientists work and thus embodies a director/spectator surrogate, later turns to social media for answers, his impatience over the lack of action potentially mirroring some viewers' own impatience.

front of their monitors, believe they are watching the usual language-teaching scenes, we, on the other hand, know we are watching a different movie: *Arrival* is now tottering on the brink of the disaster or alien war movie. The narration gives us a cognitive advantage, the opening shot revealing that the bomb is set to explode in four minutes and thirty-five seconds when Louise and Ian enter the chamber; the timer is shown on five occasions, and the sequence is actually synched to real time, the explosion occurring at 1:15:52 of the film's run time. The tension between the hard science fiction plot and the action movie subplot is dramatized through intercutting. A security detail is sent out to investigate why Marks and his crew are not responding; meanwhile, the mutineers are prepping for battle even though they clearly hope to avoid casualties. Yet again, the subplot is narrated elliptically, first with a thirty-second sequence depicting the security detail approaching the mutineers, then with the offscreen sound of gunfire, which Louise and Ian can hear from within the chamber. The subplot's elliptical and metonymical narration is enabled by the familiarity of the sci-fi action genre tropes it exploits (as in *Prisoners*, where the narration skips familiar crime-investigation moments like the rescue); it also allows the main plot focusing on the scientists' work to benefit from its dramatic thrust while retaining its status as main plot.

In the film's final act, both actors of the alien invasion narrative—the media and the military—come together to precipitate the end of the film, when media images inform both the actual and diegetic viewers (including the Montana team, whose gazes are no longer directed at their computer screens but at the television images) of General Shang's ultimatum.[40] Again, the scientific premise appears to be lagging, and the sci-fi action movie threatens to take over, Agent Halpern delivering yet another cliché: "I think our work here is done. It's in the hands of our superiors now." The narration relates the narrative split through intercutting, Louise seeing herself quitting the ongoing meeting to visit the heptapods. Media footage is followed by clichéd shots of various armies surrounding the Shells worldwide, including an *Apocalypse Now*–like shot of a helicopter rising to face a Shell (fig. 6.2). The main plot and subplot finally collide in the climax as Louise uses her scientific discovery to prevent the alien war narrative from taking over, and her success is significantly confirmed by another series of science fiction clichés: television broadcasts worldwide, followed by several Shells taking off and vanishing in the mist, like the UFOs in *Close Encounters of the First Kind* (fig. 5.2).

LINGUISTICS AS HARD SCIENCE

Arrival does not reject the dominant trends of science fiction cinema; they are accepted as primary material to be worked around (by relegating many of its tropes to the background, eliding, or debunking them) but also with (by remodeling its imagery, tapping into its dramatic energies), ultimately reinforcing the film's hard science fiction attitude, and thus distinction, through contrast. Interestingly, the science fiction clichés are not exclusively associated with the media and the military; some are voiced by the film's other scientist—the theoretical physicist, Ian Donnelly—throughout the movie. On the helicopter flight to Montana, after Colonel Weber has reiterated the scope of their mission ("Priority one: What do they want? Where are they from?"), Ian enthusiastically adds, "And beyond that, how did they get here? Are they capable of faster-than-light travel? Are they—I have a list of questions to, you know, go over, starting with a series of handshake binary sequences." Louise teasingly responds, "How about we try talking to them before we start throwing math problems at them?" Weber's reaction, "This is why you're both here," foregrounds the film's main novelty: the hard science fiction take on the alien invasion subgenre will favor the humanities rather than hard sciences. Mocking the male physicist also gives an immediate edge to the female linguist, especially since it follows Ian's hasty and arrogant demolition of the founding thesis of Louise's book in what is significantly their first exchange: "'Language is the foundation of civilization. It is the glue that holds people together. It is the first weapon to be drawn in a conflict.' The cornerstone of civilization isn't language; it's science." Louise and the film will prove the contrary or, more precisely, that linguistics is a science.

Genre clichés are consistently associated with Ian. This is notably the case in his reaction to their first visit to the Shell: a close-up captures his gloved hand reaching out to caress its surface, "the chemical composition" of which, he later states in the popular-science documentary sequence, is "unknown" (like that of Klaatu's ship and Gort the robot in *The Day the Earth Stood Still*). Ian lets out, "Yeah, that just happened," after observing the antechamber's zero gravity threshold, and he retches upon returning to the decontamination room. Even in the final act, the action movie clichés are put in Ian's mouth rather than Louise's, for instance, when he despairs, "There's gotta be a way—to get the message to them [our allies]," a line which, significantly, constitutes a sonic backdrop to Louise's oracular visions. Quite strategically, *Arrival* not only displaces the focus from astrophysics to linguistics; it positions physics alongside science fiction and action movie clichés (something the casting of MCU regular and *Bourne Legacy* star Jeremy Renner reinforces quite naturally) and linguistics on the side of a more "scientific" treatment of the premise. The male scientist, who is often the hero in classical science fiction films (*The War of the Worlds*, *Earth vs. the Flying Saucers*), is thus relegated to the status of both sidekick and genre cliché.

The slightly parodic treatment of the male scientist paves the way for the film's emphasis on linguistics as hard science and, of course, its focus on Louise Banks as the narrative's protagonist and driving force. Upon their arrival at the camp, the military setup initially abides by both genre and patriarchal standards: Weber introduces Ian Donnelly to his team first, then Louise to the linguistics team. But after their first encounter with the heptapods, Louise immediately takes over when she decides to bring a whiteboard to teach the heptapods English. Once the linguist has demonstrated what she already told the theoretical physicist in the helicopter—that science is not a universal language (unlike what the male scientists of *The Man from Planet X* and the female scientist of *Contact* believe, and what Klaatu demonstrates by helping Professor Jacob Barnhardt with his math problems in *The Day the Earth Stood Still*[41]) but is dependent on language and communication. Ian, who willingly accepts his position as assistant to the linguist, introduces himself to the heptapods as a human, then by name when Louise asks him to; enacts action verbs like "walk" (fig. 2.4.2); and deals with the computers while Louise communicates with the heptapods. Significantly, it is his voice that accompanies the montage sequence detailing their method and progress, a popular-science documentary-like sequence that is also a familiar trope of the science fiction genre (*Earth vs. the Flying Saucers* and the 1962 *Creation of Humanoids* both open with reportage sequences on UFOs). Ironically, the only scene in *Arrival* that puts the male physicist in a position of narrative authority (Louise, as we shall see, is unquestionably the film's main focalizer) is one that does little justice to his scientific credentials. Unlike Chiang's character, whose knowledge also contributes to illuminate heptapod culture,[42] the theoretical physicist is relegated to the position of performer whose job is to popularize science, putting scientific theories alongside ludicrous hypotheses ("The next most plausible theory is that Sheena Easton had a hit song at each of these sites in the 1980s. So we just don't know") and thus trivializing the seriousness of his own field. Accordingly, the second half of the documentary sequence shows him praising and explaining Louise's methods as "real" and useful science.

Taking linguistics seriously, *Arrival* seems to suggest, requires, first and foremost, making the field look serious. This is achieved by associating it with the practices and technologies usually associated with the hard sciences in science fiction cinema. Linguists are, like physicists and biologists, shown to work as a team, not only at the military camp but through their connections worldwide; the popular-science montage sequence shows Louise briefing her team but also listening to a colleague, potentially sharing his view or discovery with her. Linguists, like hard scientists, rely on machines and software, as well as on more mundane tools such as whiteboards and markers. Computer technology makes linguistics appear at once more scientific (linguistics is as scientific as the hard sciences because they all make use of the same tools) and more familiar, generically speaking (computers are a key semantic element of science fiction). The displacement of the hard sciences to the benefit of linguistics is neatly encapsulated in a variation on a common science fiction film trope (again, phase 3 in Sontag's 1965 list)[43] when Louise erases some of Ian Donnelly's equations to explain how they will reach the question, "What is your purpose on earth?" (fig. 2.4.1). Ironically, Ian's main contribution to the various discussions they have ultimately concerns a concept, the "non-zero-sum game," which is recuperated from both the military perspective (as a synonym for a trade and thus a strategy) and the linguistic one (as it turns out to be the term Hannah was looking for when questioning her mother).

Of course, it doesn't hurt that the other characters take their female colleague seriously as well. Halfway through the film, Ian repeatedly expresses his admiration for Louise ("I watch you steer us around these communication traps that I didn't even know existed") and validates the rigor of her methodology ("You approach language like a mathematician"), and in so doing, the idea that linguistics can be as serious a field as math. Colonel Weber's recognition is less forthcoming. He repeatedly demands that Louise explain the logic behind her actions, such as the use of the whiteboard to teach the heptapods how to read English or her introducing grade school words. As such, Weber embodies the representative not only of the male military but also, on a meta-level, of audiences questioning the relevance of the film's approach to the alien invasion narrative. In such scenes, Louise behaves very much like the teacher she is, facing her audience and resorting to histrionics (gestures, tone of voice, uplifted chin). As far as argumentative strategies go, she tries to adapt her framework to Weber's to make her work comprehensible, even if it means employing an analogy that isn't true (for instance, when she says that

Figures 2.4.1–2.4.2. Dr. Louise Banks erases some of Ian Donnelly's work in order to explain to Colonel Weber the necessary steps to be able to ask the heptapods, "What is your purpose on Earth?" Later, during the popular-science documentary sequence he narrates, Donnelly is shown illustrating the verb "walk," thus highlighting the male astrophysicist's limited authority as Dr. Louise Banks's assistant and temporary voice-over.

the word "kangaroo" originates in a misunderstanding of an indigenous Australian word by European colonizers). Weber's acceptance of her explanations mirrors the narrative conceit: that a potential action movie premise is being subjected to a hard science fiction treatment. Significantly, the final discussion concerns the meaning of "weapon," the military personnel relying on the lone word as proof of an imminent threat while

Louise argues, "We don't know if they understand the difference between a weapon and a tool. A language, like a culture, is messy, and sometimes one can be both." Thus, the sci-fi action movie returns when Louise and Ian are no longer able to convince their diegetic audience of the relevance of their work and, thus, of the relevance of a linguistics-based hard science fiction narrative. In cognitive terms, the scientists must maintain the other characters' "interest"—a key emotion in the "emotional structure of narrative film," which, according to Ed Tan, "depends largely on the prospect of knowledge outcomes that are charged with concerns"[44]—if they are to be allowed to try and maintain ours.

The lack of hard science fiction in film has, no doubt, to do with its presumed lack of dramatic potential. And arguably, the humanities would have even less potential than the hard sciences, whose association with technology is more apparent in science fiction and science-based films (launching into space in *Destination Moon*, computer technology in the 2014 *The Imitation Game*). The tools used by Louise thus serve an aesthetic purpose—that of visualizing and dramatizing the scientific endeavor. The digital imagery allows for connections to be drawn across the surface of the hieroglyphs, pinpointing the elements foregrounded by the scientific discourse (fig. 2.5.2)—the action playing across the surface of the screen, making visible thought processes that would otherwise remain invisible in an audiovisual medium. The scenes in which Louise is made to explain herself similarly introduce movement and tension in the thought processes that would otherwise seem intangible. Not only is her logic presented through what is ultimately a diegetic performance, but the latter is always justified by the underlying possibility that the military will terminate her mission and, in so doing, put an end to the hard science fiction plot.

The precariousness of the linguistics-based premise is especially salient in the scenes where Louise is shown working alone (by comparison, Ian is alone only when watching the news). These scenes are made exciting through dynamic camerawork and editing that energize these moments as both necessary stages in the work (on the diegetic level) and events in a dramatic continuum (on the narrative and dramatic levels). The first instance of Louise studying the soundbites they recorded, for instance, is captured by a pan from her team to her own isolated cubicle, a lateral track over her computer screen and a slow zoom-in on her studying the computer screen. The second such scene—Louise is silently annotating a hieroglyph with a red marker while consulting her computer screen (fig. 2.5.1)—uses dynamic editing (shot/reverse shot, match-on action) and rack focusing. These scenes are not elided as they tend to be in other films (even *Marooned* does not show us scientists working on their own) but remain brief, as if the film were as aware of the precariousness of the scene's role within the narrative as Louise and Ian are of theirs in relation to their mission. Such scenes are also directly juxtaposed with or overshadowed by more dramatic moments, squeezed in between the first two heptapod visits or sectioned by Louise's flashes of Hannah. This is repeated in a third sequence, in which the flashes force Louise to stop working and lead her to confide in Ian. The popular-science sequence with Ian's voice-over thus functions as the excessive version of such sequences: the scientists, the data (soundbites, hieroglyphs, dots on computer

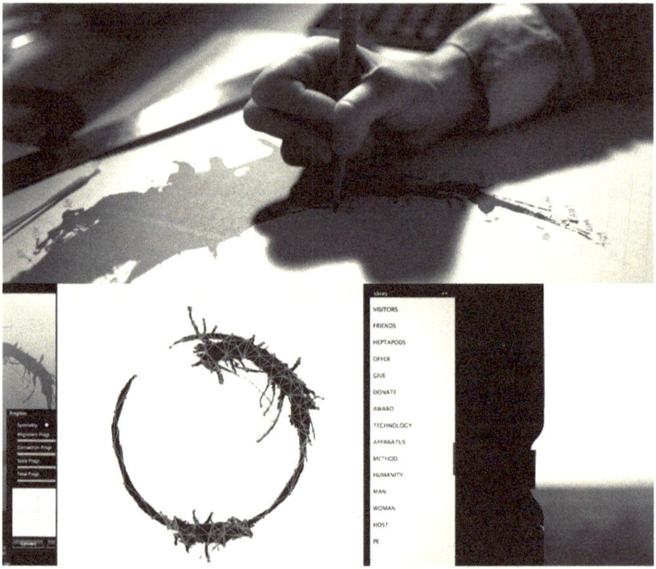

Figures 2.5.1–2.5.2. Linguistics is made serious and dramatically interesting by depicting technological imagery associated with the hard sciences in a dynamic narration.

screens), the camera (tracks, pans, tilts) are all unified by Ian's voice-over, which reprises the pedagogic function previously used by Louise when explaining to Weber, combined here with the dynamics of the media discourses that similarly occupy key positions in the film and employ montage to construct meaning.

Arrival's approach to science fiction thus strives to strike a precarious balance between sci-fi blockbuster action spectacle on the one hand and hard science fiction seriousness on the other. It is not so much about incoherently multiplying pleasures in order to "have it both ways" and maximize audience outreach,[45] as in the case of the 1990s blockbusters Geoff King discusses in *Spectacular Narratives*, although this may factor in on the marketing level (the one-minute trailer certainly concludes on an image of the explosion), as it is about attempting to channel the energies of allegedly opposed tendencies to produce an ideal and coherent synthesis, the "mainstream art" film, that would offer the best of both worlds, as in the case of the twenty-first-century films analyzed in King's more recent work. To this effect, the generic conventions of the alien invasion movie and action sci-fi are not altogether expunged but maintained, not only as a backdrop but as a potential alternative that can be channeled to momentarily reenergize the narrative and, in the end, achieve resolution through a harmonious connection to the main plot. Taking its premise seriously, *Arrival* endeavors to make linguistics dramatically interesting by simultaneously debunking the classic tropes of physics-based science fiction and mainstreaming its linguistics-based material by resorting to familiar tropes and iconography that make it engaging and comprehensible. Tensions are reflexively thematized through the interactions between the main characters' or groups' embodiment of the varied genres and attitudes of science fiction cinema. The conventions of mainstream science fiction cinema thus provide a template that does not stifle but accommodates generic experimentation.

Arrival as a Reflection on/of Communication

MAKING LANGUAGE AND COMMUNICATION THEORY INTERESTING

Communication is a recurrent science fiction theme, comprehension being an essential dramatic stake (for instance, in the 1983 *WarGames*, understanding the supercomputer WORP in order to save the world from global nuclear warfare),[1] and alien languages and technical/scientific jargon are common science fiction motifs, so much so that, in Sobchack's seminal *Screening Space: The American Science Fiction Film*, two-thirds of the chapter devoted to "the sounds of science fiction" concentrates on language and dialogue.[2] The novelty of *Arrival* lies in how it downplays the habitual emphasis on the technology of communication (satellite transmissions, encryption and translation devices, etc.) and focuses instead on the practical and theoretical problems raised when two beings who command different languages try to communicate. The film emphasizes interaction and interpretation and the "vital intercultural dimension" of translation; Dr. Banks's attempt to look "for a code based on a common experience with the heptapods" even recalls the methodology of George Lakoff–inspired pragmatics.[3] It will take the whole movie to answer the first of the "priority one" questions formulated by Colonel Weber: "What do they want?" Solving the problems that will allow the scientists to formulate these questions and comprehend their answers also requires communication between human beings. Thus, emphasis is also put on the scientists explaining their methods to the military so their plans can be greenlit (a common science fiction trope)[4] and sharing their findings with peers who don't necessarily speak the same language or share the same frameworks (a less common one), as the initial meeting between Louise and Ian proves.

Many of *Arrival*'s communication scenes between humans are staged around tables or on either side of a computer screen, an echo of the Shell chamber window, and can be contrasted to the individual spaces (Louise's cubicle, her team members' desks) in which each scientist works alone. The main filmic figure deployed to organize these scenes is, quite logically, the shot/reverse shot, a common device to dramatize dialogue in film and television. But if this device operates as the backbone of the analytical editing that governs the majority of sequences, shot sizes, angles, camera movements, and cutting techniques often vary. Lateral and back shots offset frontal shots; high and low angles counterbalance eye-level shots. Back shots of one or several characters facing a window or screen are particularly conspicuous, since they register the presence of the two parties, thus framing the communication situation as a whole. The first of Agent Halpern's onscreen discussions with his Australian counterpart comprises three shots, with a lateral medium close-up framing an over-the-shoulder shot centered on the Australian speaker on the screen; Louise's whiteboard-based linguistics lesson for Colonel Weber is exclusively dramatized by medium shot/reverse shots; and the analytical editing during the final discussion around the meeting room table is organized around a Banks-Halpern axis, with Colonel Weber representing a third apex, and alternates between medium close-ups, medium full shots, and just two establishing shots.

In the Shell chamber sequences, the variations are so frequent as to become an "intrinsic norm,"[5] with the shot/reverse shot, an "extrinsic norm" of classical narration, relegated to the status of operating as one possibility among many. Louise and Ian's second visit to the Shell utilizes a wide array of angles, as is immediately apparent from the opening shots: a high-angle shot of Louise writing "HUMAN" on the whiteboard; a lateral establishing shot of the humans in the chamber; a back shot of Weber, Louise, and Ian with the window and the two heptapods; a frontal close-up of Louise; a potential POV shot from the heptapods' perspective of the humans at the other end of the chamber; a lateral tracking long shot of Louise moving forward and repeating "human"; a three-quarter low-angle medium shot of Louise holding up the whiteboard and specifying, "I'm human. What are you?" If only one out of the five cuts is edited in shot/reverse shot, the mise-en-scène is nonetheless organized according to the axis formed by the humans on the one side and the heptapods on the other. Shot/reverse shots become more frequent (four cuts are based on the editing technique) once communication has been established through visual language, but they remain less frequent than unusual angles and inserts (of the canary, the machines, and the secondary characters' reactions). Traditional shot/reverse editing is more frequent during the third visit sequence (roughly fifteen cuts), increasing dramatically when Louise and Ian take off their masks and exchange names with the two heptapods. The final Shell chamber visits function on the same basis, with the shot/reverse shot reserved for dramatizing the heptapods' and Louise's writing (five cuts in the penultimate scene, four in the final one) and the prelude to the explosion (five cuts). The formal variations in the Shell chamber scenes set them apart from the communication scenes between humans and thus foreground them as potentially more dramatic and "interesting" (in the cognitive film studies sense of the term).

The major change made to the source novella's premise—that communication will be "face-to-face" and not mediated by a Skype-like device—has major implications that are thematic, aesthetic, and theoretical. Over the course of the first three visits to the Shell, Louise develops strategies to overcome two obstacles that impede communication. The first—when she takes the whiteboard—stems from the realization that actually speaking with the heptapods is not an option: "Look," she tells Colonel Weber when he inquires about the classroom tool, "I'm never going to be able to speak their words if they are talking. But they might have some sort of written language or basis for visual communication." Here, Louise simply reiterates what the Australian scientist admitted to Agent Halpern—that spoken language is an impasse: "We've been playing back some of their sounds. . . . Well, they play audio back at us from an unseen source. . . . It's bits of conversation from the room, random clips of dialogue. Really, we—we have nothing." *Arrival* thus shifts the novella's focus on both Heptapods A (vocal communication) and B (written communication) to the latter exclusively. If the change is justified quite rationally within the diegesis, it clearly plays to the film's more mainstream intentions: finding solutions to comprehend Heptapod A might, as in the novella, have taken much longer than the film's restricted time setting (meant to make it more "cinematic," according to Heisserer) would allow. The choice is also grounded in one of the main concerns of adaptation as a practice and a field: "medium specificity."[6] In an audiovisual medium, it may, indeed, make sense to emphasize the visual rather than the verbal. Picturing Heptapod B potentially plays into the strengths of a visual medium, and unsurprisingly, the hieroglyphs' design is an achievement Villeneuve takes great pride in.[7] The tendency to heighten the visuality of language—to transform "the word into the image," "the prosaically verbal into the prosaically visual"[8]—is also, as Sobchack has demonstrated, a science fiction cinema motif. Thus, the shot/reverse shots set an alphabet-based language in opposition to a character-based one in the chamber scenes (figs. 3.1.1–3.1.2), whereas they emphasize dialogue and verbal communication in the human discussion scenes. Finally, aesthetically speaking, the lack of interest in Heptapod A also implies that the heptapods' vocal communication will remain pure sound and that, as far as the three components of the soundtrack (voice, sound, music) are concerned, their vocalizations will remain in the realm of sound and maybe even music rather than voice, "making the aliens seem sublimely musical creatures."[9]

On her third visit, Dr. Banks does away with another communication barrier in order to encourage "reciprocity":[10] the helmet that concealed her facial expressions and muffled her voice, and the hazmat suit that constrained her movements. "They need to see me," she repeats by way of explanation. The scholar thus aims to open up the various channels of communication, adding to what linguists call the verbal the "paraverbal" (modulations of the voice) and especially the "nonverbal" (body language).[11] She then advances, touches the windowpane (fig. 3.1.3), and, having elicited a similar response from one of the heptapods, concludes, "Now that's a proper introduction." The stage is now set for Dr. Banks to go back to teaching a written language with the whiteboard. Making room for nonverbal and paraverbal communication does not just make sense theoretically and practically as a means to increase comprehension by increasing the number of communication channels; in a performance and audiovisual medium like cinema, it has clear dramatic and aesthetic potential: Louise and Ian run the risk of contamination, and both Amy Adams and Jeremy Renner will have more leeway to perform, while the audience (the heptapods and ourselves) will now have direct access to their faces and voices. Pointedly, when Louise goes back to presenting her name on the whiteboard, shot size has been reduced drastically from medium shot to medium close-up, so that her name on the whiteboard, unlike in the scene's second shot, remains offscreen and the focus is entirely on Amy Adams's face (fig. 3.1.4). The heightened presence of nonverbal and paraverbal communication involves the heptapods just as much as the humans, even if their alien features are less comprehensible. Indeed, although their cephalopod bodies remain steeped in mist and shadows, and Heptapod A remains incomprehensible to the audience and (until the end of the film) to Louise, their bodies and vocalizations express modulations to the point that we can occasionally glean some information from them: the heptapods' tentacle frantically knocking on the window as an expression of anxiety before the explosion; Costello's low moans as expressions of sorrow following the disclosure of Abbott's death.

The heptapod communication scenes remain thus configured during the film's second and third acts, with Dr. Banks

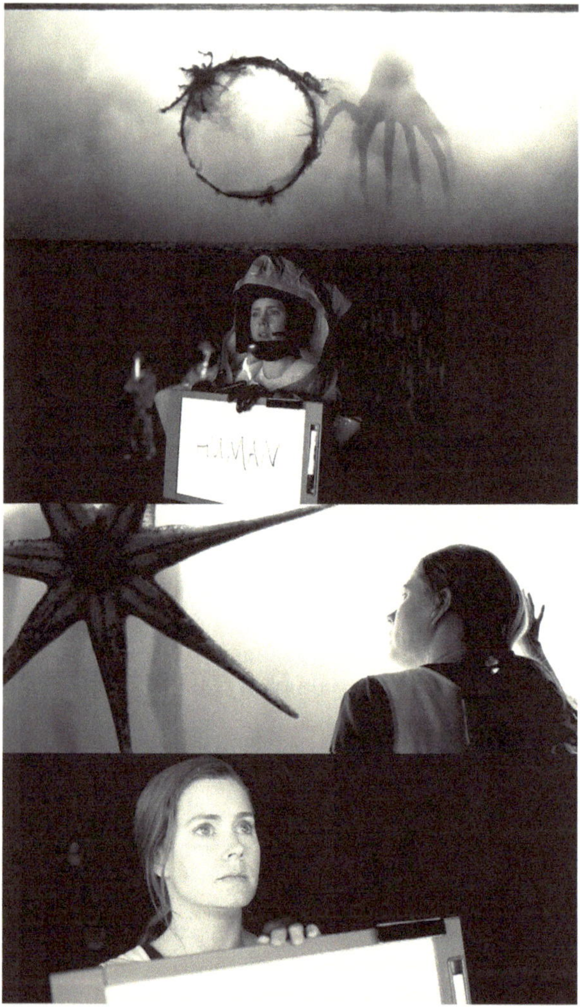

Figures 3.1.1–3.1.4. Second visit: the heptapods respond to Louise's whiteboard prompt by drawing the first hieroglyph, a significant moment that is edited in shot/reverse shot. Third visit: Louise's eliminating an obstacle to nonverbal communication with the heptapods (her hazmat suit) allows more room for Amy Adams's performance.

trading the whiteboard for more sophisticated technological tools (a digital pad and a pair of headphones), until scientific and narrative progress start to lag. The team finds itself in a new impasse when determining the meaning of the hieroglyph "Offer weapon." "We don't know if they understand the difference between a weapon and a tool," Dr. Banks explains to the military. "Our language, like our culture, is messy, and sometimes one can be both." The problem is thus one of polysemy, or what David Sutton describes as "translation across non-overlapping semantic domains," allowing the scene to "explore the classic Saussurian issue of categories."[12] The correct meaning can be deduced from linguistic context (as when we surmise the meaning of Costello's vocal reaction to Abbott's death, with Heptapod B potentially illuminating Heptapod A) and/or the cultural context in which a given language is inscribed. The last barrier that must be overcome is, therefore, not only linguistic but cultural in a very broad sense. This final problem points back to two earlier discussions Louise had with her collaborators. First, the linguist had already alerted Colonel Weber to the dangers of misinterpretation when recounting a fictitious tale about the origin of the word "kangaroo": "One of the sailors pointed at one of the animals that hopped around and put their babies in their pouch. And he asked what they were, and the Aborigine said, 'Kangaroo.' . . . It wasn't till later that they learned that kangaroo means 'I don't understand.'" The mythical tale suggests that language and communication in general are culturally determined: the misunderstanding of a word that expresses misunderstanding actually stems from the misunderstanding of that which the white colonizer believed to be a universal gesture but which could be understood differently by someone from another culture. Ironically, Dr. Banks, who is well aware of the nature of this semantic origin tale, will use the same universal gesture on her third visit.

Louise finally figures out the meaning of the word "weapon," and thus obtains the answer to the question she was hired for, when the final frontier is eliminated: the window that separates the humans from the heptapods. The space Louise shares with Costello on her last visit is not just physical; it is also linguistic and cultural. It is appropriate from both a generic and a dramatic perspective that the word that poses a problem is "weapon," since it is the tool that is feared in alien invasion movies. But the final revelation that the weapon is actually a language also harks back to the hard-versus-soft-science-as-foundation-of-civilization debate with which Ian awkwardly broke the ice with Louise in the helicopter. The final revelation seems to prove Dr. Banks right—that language is, in fact, the foundation of civilization, or at the least, that linguistics is a science. It could also demonstrate that the film, like the story, is, in effect, filtered through the perspective of the post-heptapod-encounter Louise, which would thus have informed, rather than confirmed, her thesis that language is "the first weapon drawn in a conflict," a thesis that neatly encapsulates the film's own modus operandi: exploiting various theories in order to make the first-contact communication problem both comprehensible and dramatically interesting for a wide variety of audiences.

A METADISCOURSE ON SPECTATORSHIP

It likely didn't escape anybody's attention—certainly not actor Jeremy Renner's[13]—that the window separating the heptapods from the humans in the Shell chamber resembles a movie screen (the massive white screen was lit up by forty thousand lightbulbs placed behind it).[14] Bertrand Gervais even compares the screen to the Google search box.[15] One of the notable changes from Chiang's story, the window/screen has obvious reflexive potential in a visual medium, inviting parallels, Tijana Mamula argues, with black-and-white cinema, which the renaming of the heptapods after slapstick stars Abbott and Costello (instead of Chiang's Flapper and Raspberry) certainly reinforces.[16] The screen's blazing whiteness chromatically dominates the multiple establishing shots of the dark rectangular chamber regardless of the angle (fig. 3.2.1), even in the POV shots from the heptapods' perspective, in which the light illuminates the human figures (fig. 3.2.2). The analogy is reinforced by the chamber's design; the walls, floor, and ceiling are bare, while the long antechamber leading to it and the walls' irregular mineral surface bring to mind Plato's cave, which provided the basis for Jean-Louis Baudry's 1975 theory of the cinematic apparatus as inducing a regressive, dream-like state in the "prisoner-spectators" that dominant ideologies (namely capitalism) can then exploit.[17]

The analogy is, from the outset, driven in by the position occupied by the Shell's occupants and visitors: the heptapods provide the spectacle onscreen, the wide-eyed humans represent the audience watching them, bathed in the light emitted by the window. The act of watching is occasionally expressed through POV shots through Louise's visor (fig. 3.2.3) and mediated by the humans' reliance on technology to view and record the interactions, an activity the narration underscores by repeatedly showing Captain Marks's camera, positioned in front of the other soldiers, and by using occasional insert close-ups of the monitors and decibel meters. During the popular-science documentary sequence, the extreme close-up of the camera lens with the heptapods' reflection in it (fig. 3.2.4) encapsulates the whole setup by turning the recording device into a screen, the actual creature into a spectral image. Of course, the heptapods' reflection reflexively draws attention to its "nature" as a CGI creation, and thus as a digital image, an assortment of pixels without a referent, matter without corporeality. The diegetic recording setup thus highlights the production of such science fiction imagery[18] and, in the process, the illusionist power of cinema discussed by Baudry in the writings that initiated apparatus theory.

During the first visit and on a first viewing, the Shell chamber is, in effect, a fairly elementary mise en abyme of *Arrival*,[19] with two of the diegetic viewers (and the actual audience) discovering the heptapods (and the VFX) at the same time. But the allegory of spectatorship is reconfigured as the narrative evolves. For one, the audience members' positions are modified. On the first visit, the humans are organized into three clearly distinct groups, spatially speaking: Louise, Ian, and Weber in the midground, Captain Mars and the other soldiers recording the events in the background, and the rest of the staff back at the base. In terms of activity, however, the differences in each member's experience are slight: all of them are watching—the first-timers are just more overwhelmed by the experience than the rest of the audience. For Louise and Ian at least, the first visit very much resembles the experience film critics and scholars like Allison Griffiths commonly describe as "immersion," that is, "the sensation of entering a space that immediately identifies itself as somehow separate from the world."[20] The oceanic metaphor is evoked when they plunge

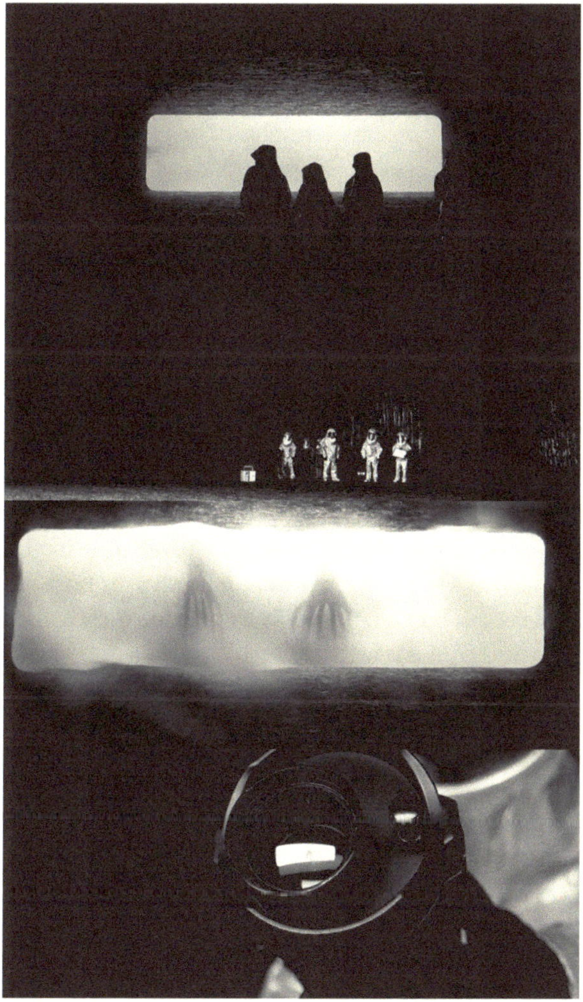

Figures 3.2.1–3.2.4. The Shell chamber as metaphor for the cinematic apparatus, with the human audience bathed in the light emanated by the gleaming white window. Next, a POV shot through Dr. Banks's hazmat visor, and, finally, Captain Marks's camera lens reflecting the CGI-produced spectacle.

into the dark antechamber in their suits and furthered by the heptapods' giant squid-like appearance.[21] Although the human characters remain separated from the heptapods by a window, the power of the spectacle is such that it overwhelms them physically (Louise clenches her fist; Ian vomits in the decontamination room), emotionally (Louise seems panicky), and presumably imaginatively. The narration insists on the immersive quality of the experience by registering Louise's reactions in close shots and decreasing shot size so as to seemingly penetrate the mist beyond the window by eliminating the frame, concluding in a back shot of Louise with her head framed by the two heptapods in the background.

On the second visit, Louise deliberately reconfigures the setup by stepping away from the rest of her group and attempting to communicate with the heptapods using the whiteboard, while the heptapods' inky response reconfigures the window, transforming it into their own silvery whiteboard. Though still at a remove (Louise is wearing her hazmat suit and remains at a distance from the screen), the spectacle is something she no longer merely views but consciously interacts with, and Louise is no longer the passive spectator of apparatus theory but the active spectator of cognitive film studies, as theorized by David Bordwell and others—a hermeneutist who "comes armed and active to the task,"[22] striving to interpret the images onscreen. But in so doing, she has also stepped onto the stage and become a performer, as highlighted by a lateral tracking shot when she breaks away from the diegetic audience. The shift is foregrounded by the scene's opening shot (Louise writing the word "HUMAN" on the whiteboard) and closing shots: the back shot of Louise framed by the heptapods, similar to the one that closed the first Shell visit scene, is followed by medium close-ups of Louise, Ian, and Weber reacting to the interaction.

The third visit opens on an ensemble shot of a group of soldiers facing the monitoring screens in the military base, soon joined by Colonel Weber, who is then shown in a back shot framed by several screens. Weber's shift from accompanying Louise and Ian in the chamber (and thus on the set) to following their progress on the monitors (like a TV director in the editing room) confirms that the spectacle is no longer limited to the heptapods (shown on the screen to his right) but to their interactions with the scientists (shown on the screen to his left), thus to the chamber as a whole. Even before Louise penetrates the inside of the Shell, she, as Vincent Jaunas would have it, has effectively gone from operating like a spectator to a performer/screenwriter/director,[23] who is again shown writing her name and now pointing at the heptapods to distribute the floor, while Ian at her side acts like a performer and assistant director (the documentary sequence will later show him adjusting the machines and being directed by Louise to teach the heptapods the meaning of the verb "walk"). By casting off her suit and stepping forward to touch the window during the third visit, Louise seeks to enter a tactile relationship with the heptapods. A lateral establishing shot shows her dwarfed by the convex window, introducing a surprising sense of depth, since previous establishing shots emphasized the window's flatness (fig. 3.3.1). This is shortly followed by an extreme close-up of her right hand touching its surface (fig. 3.3.2). Because such close-ups were previously reserved for recording machines (screens, decibel meters), the emphasis is now on the shift from one-way audiovisual communication (recording) to a tactile two-way interaction involving the nonverbal and the paraverbal. Louise here represents embodied spectatorship, as theorized by Laura U. Marks and Vivian Sobchack, for whom "the film experience is meaningful *not to the side of our bodies but because of our bodies*";[24] her experience exemplifies more contemporary views of immersion, Allison Griffiths's definition also positing that the process "eschews conventional modes of spectatorship in favor of a more bodily participation in the experience."[25] Of course, although the heptapod tentacle is physical within the diegesis, it remains a digital image, as the reflection in the camera lens reflexively recalls.

The shift in viewer positions is characteristic of many cinematic mises en abyme that function as allegories of spectatorship —*Rear Window* (Hitchcock, 1954) is a classic example[26]— but it is systematized in *Arrival,* because each visit introduces a particular viewing position (immersion, hermeneutics, embodiedness). Although the film appears to describe a progression from a 1970s to a 1980s/early 1990s and then to a twenty-first-century view of spectatorship, the progression is actually more cumulative than evolutionary. The repetition of back shots of Louise and Ian framed by the frameless window, sometimes even as they are addressing the diegetic audience or the heptapods or reading or writing a hieroglyph, indicates that cognitive activity precludes neither visual immersion nor embodied involvement but, rather, that they can potentially function simultaneously and on multiple levels. This is confirmed by Louise's final visit inside the Shell, when the mise en abyme makes way for an "intradiegetic metalepsis";[27] the transgression of the ontological boundary between human and heptapod is foregrounded by the lack of explanation as to how Louise can inexplicably survive in the heptapod atmosphere the window had previously separated the humans

Figures 3.3.1–3.3.4. Third visit: having rid herself of her hazmat suit, Louise Banks approaches the convex window and presses her hand to the pane. Final visit: now fully immersed inside the alien atmosphere beyond the screen, Louise's experience continues to be manifold—immersion, tactile, cognitive.

from. Allegorically, Louise has, as in *The Purple Rose of Cairo* (1985), crossed the movie screen[28]—the frame provided by the chamber has disappeared, and she is always inside the heptapods' space regardless of the shot angle—and her experience combines all three modes of spectatorship: she is simultaneously immersed in a gaseous environment; flooded by visions emerging from within her mind, her hair floating and her eyes struggling to stay open; and yet still trying to comprehend the meaning of the word "weapon" and grasp the ink (figs. 3.3.3–3.3.4). The film's accumulation of mises en abyme lays a claim to the richness of the spectatorial experience even in a VFX-dependent blockbuster.

NARRATION AS COMMUNICATION

The diegetic scenes of spectatorship thematize what the film's narration explores through its own devices: the idea that film *is* communication. Tijana Mamula has argued that *Arrival* offers a reflection on film language; in equating Heptapod B with cinema, the film posits a nostalgic view of film as a universal language capable of reconfiguring human perception, reminiscent of the theories expounded in early writings on cinema by the likes of Béla Balázs and Jean Epstein.[29] The link between language and art is evoked early on in a special communication situation in which Dr. Banks begins her lecture in an amphitheater with a very low attendance: "Today, we are talking about Portuguese, and why it sounds so different from the other Romance languages. The story of Portuguese begins in the kingdom of Galicia, in the Middle Ages, where language was seen as an expression of art." Her statement obviously foreshadows the singular beauty of the heptapods' hieroglyphs, but it also invites consideration of the relationship between language and art. It raises age-old questions—Can language be art? Is art a language?—while her use of the term "expression" posits a communication act whereby someone expresses something (to someone else) through art/language. To human eyes, the hieroglyphs resemble abstract works of art, and interpreting them requires in-depth analysis of each detail, as when Louise works to identify segments (fig. 2.5).

There is nothing particularly novel about the idea that art or cultural products imply an act of communication. Reader response theory has long modeled the relationship between reader and text on communication. The opening lines of the preface to Wolfgang Iser's 1978 *The Act of Reading* state that "it is presumed that the literary work is an act of communication," that "the formation of the text is a set of instructions," and that "the meaning of the text is something [the reader] has to assemble."[30] Twenty years later, Jean-Jacques Lecercle described the creation of a text or an interpretation as a "situation of communication" whose "dialogic exchanges" his Author-Language-Text-Encyclopedia-Reader model seeks to account for.[31] Film theorists have long used the dubious term "cinematic language" to refer to "the signifying figures that are specific to cinema" and described cinema as a hermetic form of communication that precludes exchanges with the audience, whose members can respond only after the fact through interpretive acts.[32] In his 1985 *Narration in the Fiction Film*, David Bordwell rejects the facile transposition of communication models to describe the experience of film and argues that film narration does not imply the presence of a narrator, but he does make a case for the "communicativeness" of film narration and seeks to account for how the spectator comprehends the story thanks to the narration.[33] Language, of course, plays an integral part in the comprehensibility of film narration, in the form of dialogue, voice-overs, and titles, the advent of the sound film having rapidly placed both the voice and the word at the center of the soundtrack, making cinema both "vococentric" and "verbocentric."[34]

A first-contact film that follows a linguist trying to make sense of an alien language, *Arrival* is a prime example of a voco- and verbocentric film, as the wordy communication scenes analyzed above prove. And yet, it also celebrates what Bordwell calls the "omnicommunicativeness" of audiovisual narration, cinema's "multilingualism,"[35] or what linguists and communication theorists would now call multimodality, that is, "how different kinds of meaning making are combined into an *integrated, multimodal whole*."[36] *Arrival* notably reminds us that a film can still, as in the days of silent cinema, do without dialogue. Significantly, Louise's decision to try and use a whiteboard is conveyed through the narration without recourse to speech: a low-angle three-quarter close-up of Adams looking blankly in front of her depicts the character's sense of being at a loss as to what to do until she notices something offscreen; a low-angle over-the-shoulder shot reveals a whiteboard in the blurry left background, rack focusing from foreground to background, thereby mimicking Louise's own shift in attention (fig. 3.4). It is only once Louise is fully suited up outside that she explains her intentions to Colonel Weber when he inquires about the whiteboard. The scene thus demonstrates the power of film narration as visual communication at the very moment when Louise decides to take a "visual aid" that is, quite ironically, also a linguistic one; it relies on our ability to actively infer meaning based on our combined knowledge of

Figure 3.4. Louise Banks's decision to resort to the whiteboard is narrated wordlessly through a simple eyeline match.

real-world behaviors and the norms of classical narration such as the eyeline match (as in Bordwell's theory of narration) and, ultimately, to fill in the "blanks" (as in Iser's theory of reader response): "Whenever the reader bridges the gaps," Iser posits, "communication begins."[37]

The alien invasion action movie subplot is narrated along similar lines, relying, as we have seen, on our own familiarity with the genre. It is first made manifest visually when the narration shifts from a medium close-up of Louise following her first vision of Hannah to an establishing shot of her framed by two unidentified onlookers, who are then shown glancing at each other in a reverse close shot (fig. 2.3.2). The subplot is thus introduced nonverbally through a shift in focalization and the glances the male actors direct at each other in order to express secret complicity. For the audience, it is only with hindsight that the meaning becomes obvious. Similar silent complicity recurs when the narration cuts to a lateral medium close-up of Marks and another soldier preparing the attack on the Montana Shell, looking at each other while loading the pickup; the scene concludes on a medium close-up of Marks casting a wary glance toward the base, presumably expressing concern that their plot will be found out before they have carried it out or, perhaps, momentary doubt regarding the mutiny's righteousness. The soldiers' muteness serves an obvious dramatic purpose—it confirms the subplot's secondariness while instilling a sense of threat and building up a dramatic contrast with the final explosion—but it is justified diegetically by the military's own mode of communication: in a battle situation, soldiers communicate nonverbally through looks and gestures. This is demonstrated once again during the climax, when the soldiers are searching the base for Louise and use the habitual gestures (pointing, holding up two fingers) audiences have grown accustomed to thanks to war movies. All these instances involve what is, on the diegetic level, nonverbal communication, but they are very much an integral part of the film narration. Such moments are singled out and made meaningful not only by framing and cutting but also by staging; this essential element of film narration, as Bordwell frequently reminds us, appears unremarkable because, as in other performance arts, it works to "naturalize" both setting and body language, collapsing the fictional gestures used by the characters to communicate within the scene with those used by the actors to render narrative elements and character psychology comprehensible to the audience.[38]

The "omnicommunicativeness" of film narration can also become uncommunicative and impede narrative comprehension in order to convey ambiguity. An early instance occurs upon Louise's return to the base after her third visit, when she receives an injection in the medical ward (figs. 3.5.1–3.5.3). A canted high-angle three-quarter close-up of her face with

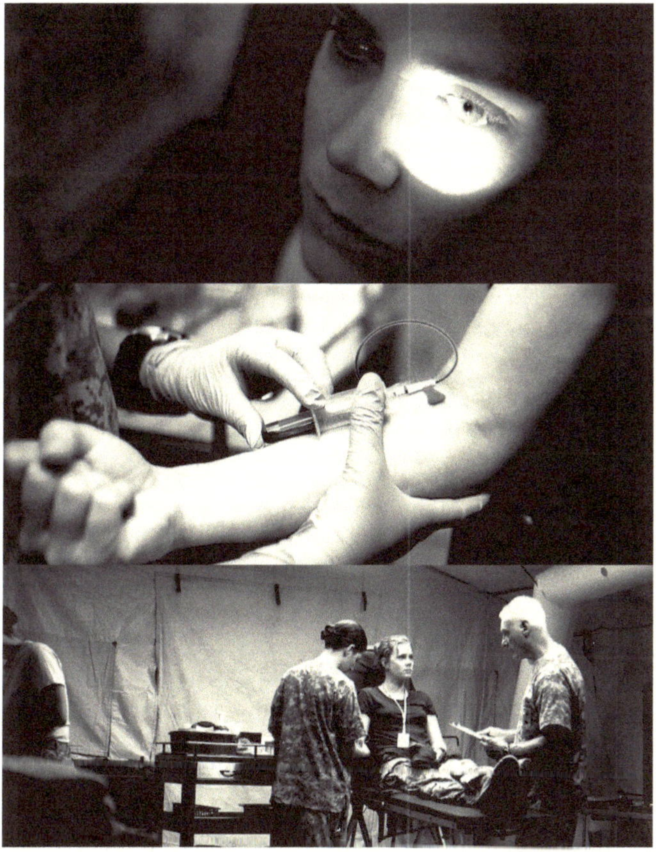

Figures 3.5.1–3.5.3. Upon a medical examination following Louise's third visit to the Shell chamber, a close-up associated with the male doctor's offscreen voice introduces uncertainty regarding whose hand is injecting a serum into Louise's arm, a momentary confusion that foreshadows Louise's more radical visions to come.

a pencil light being shined into her right eye is accompanied by Dr. Kettler's voice offscreen and followed by a close-up of her right arm as someone (whose surgical gloved hands can be seen) takes her blood. Dr. Kettler's referring to the blood test suggests a correlation between voice and action, and thus that the hands in the close-up are his own. But a medium full shot then reveals that the person taking the blood sample is actually the nurse on Louise's right and that Dr. Kettler is on her left. The narration thus destabilizes classical conventions along with our expectations, because the hands in the shot are not correlated to the voice; here, we have been duped by our own vococentric view of cinema. Of course, such ambiguity remains "communicative," since it is meant to alert us to the alterations in Louise's perception now that she has exposed herself to the heptapods (hence the unusual angles).

This sets the tone for the third act, when Louise's visions are similarly conveyed through facial expressions (Heisserer insists that Amy Adams's ability to "show in her performance in her body language what she's thinking" is one of the main reasons she was cast),[39] gestures, and images rather than verbal language (pointedly, Louise refrains from mentioning her visions to her colleagues). The visions not only upset the character, they introduce breaks in the film narration. Like the blood sample scene in which Louise's discomfort is first made manifest, they play on the disjunction between voices on the one hand and bodies and images on the other. The disjunction is epitomized in the Sapir-Whorf hypothesis discussion scene, which turns out to be a dream sequence. The scene opens with an image of a heptapod floating in its gaseous environment accompanied by Ian's voice, a moment that becomes acceptable by classical standards as a sound bridge between two scenes once the actual source of the voice is confirmed as Ian in the subsequent shot. The narration then proceeds to completely upset our comprehension of narrative space: the editing violates the 180-degree rule; the staging ignores its own terms (Louise addresses Ian in front of her, then to her right); and the sequence concludes on a reverse shot of Louise's interlocutor as now being a heptapod, a nod to the finale of *Enemy* when the protagonist finds a giant spider in place of his double's wife. Retrospectively, the entire sequence was, in effect, illustrating the Sapir-Whorf hypothesis, not merely through dialogue but through disconnections between various communication channels.

The predominance of visions and sounds over dialogue is asserted at the dawn of the final act. During the tense discussion between the scientists and the military that paves the way for the climax, the focus shifts from Louise's attempt to convince the military to her struggle to make sense of her visions. Once the visions erupt, the narration remains centered on her face in extreme close-up, while the men are relegated offscreen or to the blurry background. Ironically, the dialogue remains focused on a communication problem—how to send a message to the other landing sites to avoid global war—but the framing makes it clear that it is what the visions/visuals are showing us that is of import, not the voices and words, so that the continued presence of dialogue and the return to the men in the room conclude on the failure of this discussion and, more generally, of their mission. The male voices occupy, quite artificially, the center of the soundtrack but are divested of their role as primary provider of narrative information; it is in the visuals, as in the hieroglyphs, that meaning is to be found, suggesting "that *Arrival* believes in the dominance of the image."[40]

Like the story it is based on, *Arrival* is not content with depicting scientists hard at work trying to communicate with each other and the military to solve a communication problem; its dramatization of the process is grounded in some of the basic tenets of contemporary linguistics, emphasizing various forms of communication and the importance of context, and endeavoring to make the problems, hurdles, and methods engaging. Communication is not just the film's main theme; on a meta-level, it is a means to interrogate film spectatorship and an audiovisual medium like cinema. Not only do the chamber visit scenes develop a historiography of film spectatorship theory—from passive to active, cognitive to corporeal engagement—they also suggest that the levels of spectatorial engagement are as varied as the means by which we communicate and make meaning. One mode does not preclude another; rather, they occur together. *Arrival* is ultimately a celebration of the power of an audiovisual medium like cinema to welcome diversity and disjunction; in this respect, at least, the narration does not assert the sense of wholeness implicit in the universal language thesis the diegesis seems to uphold, as Mamula would have it,[41] but contests it. Indeed, exclusive focus on the hieroglyphs is not just a clever adaptation strategy playing the medium specificity card; it allows the film to experiment with the omnicommunicativeness of film narration, illustrating contemporary theories of multimodality. In steering a course that aims to combine the pleasures of blockbuster and art cinema, *Arrival* refuses to sacrifice dramatic interest to its own lofty ambitions, while attempting to elicit spectatorial involvement on several levels, whether asking us to recognize the mise en abyme or putting our inductive capacities to the test by requiring us to fill in the blanks.

Arrival as an Experience of Time

ULTIMATUMS, THE NEWS, AND THE TEMPORALITY OF SCIENCE

The change made to the source text's title, with an "arrival" replacing an entire "life," would tend to suggest that time is less central to the film than to the novella, yet the reference to time remains implicit in the reference to an action that is temporary. The 2016 film offers, in effect, an exploration of the many relations between time and cinema: time is one of the narrative's central themes (the Montana team is working on a deadline, General Shang's ultimatum); it plays a structuring role (via the flashback structure); and it can be experienced on various levels—cognitive, memory, sensitive—that the film endeavors to express.

Time in *Arrival* is not necessarily relative, but it is definitely a question of framework. While the story reveals that heptapods and humans have radically different relations to time, it is clear from the outset that one's apprehension of time can vary. Even if time is conceived as linear, chronological, causal, and of the essence for the media, military, and scientists, the nature of the relation to time differs from one group to another, and these views may conflict. The military and politicians aim to speedily resolve a crisis and operate on the assumption that there is no time, while scientists need time to carry out their research, as the slow science movement has been advocating since the publication of Isabelle Stengers's 2018 manifesto. For the news media, whose relation to time is grounded in economics, "timeliness," "immediacy," "consequence," "suspense," and "progress" are essential criteria for gauging what will make the news:[1] the novel event should be happening now and have potential effects on the consumers' present and future.

In *Arrival*, the alien encounter is narrated in an eminently linear fashion, with the media establishing a calendar of events: Alien Crisis Days 4, 5, 25, 27, and 28 are mentioned. A well-known science fiction and disaster movie convention that Heisserer's directorial debut *Hours* had already made use of, the news media sequences play a structuring role and articulate the dramatic tension by instilling a sense of urgency at key moments. The TV news serves to introduce the inciting event (the arrival) and the climax precipitated by China's declaration of war (Day 27), and it marks the turning points that lead into acts 2 (Day 4) and 3 (Day 25). An NRCN news sequence specifies the duration of the ellipsis—twenty days—providing more specific information in that regard than the popular-science documentary sequence, which had summed up the progress made in "a month"; immediately following a calm, intimate exchange between Louise and Ian, the news sequence comes as a reminder that tension is escalating on a global scale and that time remains of the essence.

Exploiting the contemporary news media's main goal—to report interesting and potentially dramatic information—such scenes operate as markers of the film's dramatic tension.

Clearly, the first and last days of the alien crisis are the most interesting within the diegetic world and possibly for some audience members. At Louise Banks's university, all eyes are riveted on the news, whether on shared or individual screens. The event is first experienced as mediated, with the Shells glimpsed on television screens in the background, like the creatures in Gareth Edwards's *Monsters* (2010) and *Godzilla* (2014). Yet the news event is so powerful as to shatter both a group's and an individual's relation to time; Louise "dismisse[s]" her class and spends the next forty-eight hours riveted to the news. The changing light in her house indicates the passing of time, while the television maintains a continuous sonic backdrop, with two sound bridges allowing scenes to smoothly segue into the next. The news media backdrop is interrupted only by Louise's phone call with her mother and her walking across a deserted campus. At the military base, the news and social media continue to garner some attention; they remain relevant even for people on the front line, at the least as an indicator of what is going on nation- and worldwide. Agent Halpern studies the media to assess the geopolitical situation, while lower-ranking officers like Captain Marks seem to turn to the media in search of answers the higher-ranking officers and scientists are failing to provide. The renewed presence of the media in the third act is synonymous with the fact that the scientists are not progressing fast enough, harking back to Colonel Weber's opening remark to Louise Banks: "Two days. And already the public expects us to know the answers." Previously relegated to the background, the screen featuring the NRCN news report now occupies the whole frame, and the diegetic viewer turns out to be neither Marks nor an anonymous soldier, but Ian Donnelly himself. Once the global network among scientists has been shut down, even the higher-ranking officers and scientists turn to the news, whose images occupy the whole frame and bookend the sequence. The news has caught up with them. The precariousness of the event as depicted by the news media operates as a mise en abyme of the precariousness of the hard science fiction premise: the ongoing arrival plot is threatened by stasis, while the apocalyptic finale threatens to put an end to the film.

While the news media provides a structuring backdrop and marks the return of the alien invasion movie as an action-packed genre in the third and final acts, from the outset the main premise sets two dramatically different relations to time in opposition to each other. The popular-science documentary sequence, which opens with a list of "the many things [the scientists] don't know about heptapods," suggests that, for scientists, "a month" is basically the equivalent of Colonel Weber's "two days." As Louise and Ian's main interlocutor, it is the colonel's role to act as a constant reminder that they are running out of time: he seeks Louise out because she made "quick work" of her last translation, allows her ten minutes to pack a bag before the helicopter takes off, says that the medical procedure upon arrival will "take just a few minutes," that she and Ian have "till 0200 hours to figure something out" upon their return from their first visit, that Louise's new plan to teach the heptapods how to speak and read has "got to take longer," and, on Day 26, that "ready or not," they "need to ask [the heptapods] the big question." Forest Whitaker's no-nonsense tone and elocution stress this sense of urgency, in particular whenever he asks the scientists to explain their methods to him. All military personnel try to keep the scientists working around the clock; Marks tells Ian and Louise to "hurry up" before their first visit, and Agent Halpern, who is first introduced discussing a temporal paradox regarding the oxygen in the Shell's atmosphere with his Australian counterpart, is the one to terminate the mission: "I think our work here is done." Significantly, the adverb "now" is used predominantly by the military (Weber, Halpern, Doctor Kettler, anonymous radio voices), by the media, and by Louise when she interacts with Weber ("What happens now?") or attempts to obtain the information the military requires ("Give technology now"). The soundtrack further conveys this sense of urgency in the form of a siren, which announces the opening of the Shell in fifteen minutes, a fact Weber relays to Louise at the end of the scene where he introduces her to her team, right before a radio voice starts initiating a countdown ("T minus 14 minutes to Shell access," "T minus 9 minutes to Shell access"). In the third act, a different siren resounds when the international network has been disconnected. This culminates, as we have seen, with the time bomb set by the mutineers, which puts an end to Louise and Ian's repeated visits and, finally, with the turning point leading to act 4, General Shang's "ultimatum" to the invaders.

The scientists value duration above the military's need for immediate action. Weber's and the military's acting like time is something that can be compressed and bargained over, that it is merely a matter of economy (physical and linguistic), is offset right after the first visit, when Ian asks military personnel taking off his suit "to wait just a minute" so he can regain his composure. If the popular-science documentary sequence opens with a host of unanswered questions, Ian's voice-over transitions to the scientists' successes—"Louise is putting us all to shame"—using the progressive form in order to evoke "duration" and "incompleteness" and to construe research as a "process."[2] Entitled "Kangaru" in reference to Louise's phony lesson about misunderstanding an indigenous Australian word, the musical piece accompanying the sequence comprises parallel lines of repeated notes played in the key of D-sharp major and produced by bubbly feminine voices, expressing repetition as a positive energy–filled quality. The fact that taking one's time is not a luxury but a necessity for conducting solid research is yet again evoked when Ian explains that Louise believes "it could take another month" to expand the heptapods' vocabulary. When the military starts worrying about the meaning of the phrase "Offer weapon," Louise's solution is to "go back in." "Quick work" is not the rule in science and is possible only once knowledge has been acquired (Louise's ability to translate languages she is familiar with, like Farsi and Mandarin). Even Ian ends up lamenting the slowness of science when he concludes that "it's going to take [them] years" to make sense of the multitude of hieroglyphs. The temporal structure of *Arrival* is thus an impossible Chinese box wherein immediacy, urgency, and economy (the media, the military, and possibly "the public") strive to compress duration (science); the simple present strives to contain the progressive form, a pressure that is manifest in the increasing use of the word "now" in the final act and, again, in Whitaker's vocal performance.

MIND-GAME FILM AND TEMPORAL PARADOX

There is nothing particularly original about a "puzzle" or "mind-game" film made in 2016. Complex narratives became popular in the 1990s following the success of *Groundhog Day* (Ramis, 1993) and *Pulp Fiction* (Tarantino, 1994),[3] with directors like David Lynch and Christopher Nolan practically specializing in them, and Villeneuve already indulging in intertwining storylines in *Maëlstrom* (2000), *Polytechnique* (2009), and *Incendies* (2010). The phenomenon drew critical attention from the likes of David Bordwell (2006), Warren Buckland (2009), and Thomas Elsaesser (2009, 2021). Unlike network films such as *Nashville* (Altman, 1975), *Short Cuts* (Altman, 1993), *Kansas City* (Altman, 1996), *Magnolia* (Anderson, 1999), *21 Grams* (Iñárritu, 2003), *Crash* (Haggis, 2004), and *Babel* (Iñárritu, 2006), which are organized according to "the connectedness of apparently random phenomena"[4] and aim to offer a kaleidoscopic view of a given social milieu, puzzle films, says Buckland, "blur the boundaries between different levels of reality, are riddled with gaps, deception, labyrinthine structures, ambiguity, and overt coincidences"; their "complexity . . . operates on two levels: narrative and narration."[5] Both terms ("puzzle" and "mind-game") posit a view of the film as a game with the spectators, in which they are misled and must deal with the omissions and misdirections created by the narrative,[6] but the mind-game film's "core" feature is that it "revolve[s] around mentally unstable characters."[7] In the mind-game film, complex narrative and narration are thus expressions of the protagonist's subjectivity and often pathology. Films like *Pulp Fiction*, *Inception*, and *Dunkirk* (Nolan, 2017) thus qualify as puzzle films, while *Lost Highway* (Lynch, 1997), *Memento*, *Mulholland Dr.* (Lynch, 2001), *Donnie Darko* (Kelly, 2001), and *Inland Empire* (Lynch, 2006) are also mind-game films.

Elsaesser evokes *Arrival* in his discussion of the mind-game film. With "its language without tenses,"[8] *Arrival* does include many features of what he describes as a "mode or tendency" rather than a "genre."[9] Buckland lists the characteristics identified by Elsaesser as follows:

> (1) the protagonist (and spectator) participates in unusual events, whose structures does not follow cause-effect logic/linear progression; (2) a deluded protagonist who cannot distinguish between fantasy and reality (and their experience is shared with the spectator); (3) the protagonist has a friend who turns out to be imaginary; (4) the protagonist questions his/her own identity and existence; (5) the narrative undergoes a dramatic plot twist; (6) the protagonist is plagued by delusions about the disappearance of a child.[10]

The specificity of *Arrival* is that, like *Donnie Darko*, it is not framed as a mind-game film from the outset. Some of the common features identified by Elsaesser (points 2, 3, 4, and 6) start to appear only halfway through the narrative, when Louise starts having visions (of Hannah or of Ian and the heptapod in her sleeping quarters), while others (points 1 and 5) are reserved for the climax. So the first level of *Arrival*'s game lies in realizing that it is, in effect, a mind-game film. On a first viewing, the narrative appears linear until it is revealed that Louise is seeing the future and not the past: the "dramatic plot twist" (5) is that the events do not follow a "linear progression" (1). As Bordwell points out, the adapters' not retaining the modal verb "will" employed by Ted Chiang's narrator to refer to the future in the film's opening voice-over transforms the novella's "premise" into a "reveal."[11] The events related in the prologue—the death of Louise Banks's child, Hannah—seem to have taken place before the heptapods' arrival and fulfill the function of providing us with the heroine's background and aligning us "with Louise by sharing her affective states, her

Figures 4.1.1–4.1.2. The chromatic unity of the melancholy view from Louise's living room functions as a lure, leading us to posit continuity between her life before the heptapods' arrival and after Hannah's birth.

deep sadness and grief."[12] This interpretation is reinforced by the unity of space, which incites us to take the unity of time for granted as well; during the first days of the alien invasion, Louise is living alone in the same house she shared with her daughter, with a view of a body of water that tends to blend in with the overcast sky in a uniformly gray landscape (figs. 4.1.1–4.1.2). Implicitly, Louise's bereavement even provides psychological motivation: not only is she free to fly off with Weber on a moment's notice, but the mission can provide the "emotionally numb" character with a welcome change of scene.[13]

The likelihood of Louise's situation is reinforced by one of the major adaptational changes brought to the novella: Hannah dies at a much younger age, so Louise would presumably have changed less in a ten-year interval than in a twenty-year one.

On a first viewing, we interpret subsequent references to Louise's personal life with this background in mind. For us, the little girl in her visions is obviously her daughter, and Louise's admission to Ian that she is "single" is all the more poignant as it recalls that she seems to have faced her daughter's passing all alone. The mental images that erupt halfway through the film and mark the beginning of the third act thus appear unmistakably as flashbacks. These inserts, like those in other contemporary films,[14] exploit few of the trope's classical markers, apart from the "changes in image qualities" and "in elements of mise en scène," and retain instead what Maureen Turim qualifies as modernist "disjunction," which "restor[es] some of the energy of dislocation and mimesis of thought and memory inherent in the flashback."[15] An arsenal of devices is, however, deployed to express these flashes,[16] constituting a poetics that is also mobilized to depict K's and Paul Atreides's visions in *Blade Runner 2049* and *Dune: Part One*. Handheld close-ups and medium close-ups cling to the subject's body and express the visceral quality of memory, that remembrance is an embodied experience; back lighting, lens flare, and the blur produced by shallow focus composition evoke the precariousness and fleetingness of these images (fig. 4.2.1); the use of cuts instead of lap dissolves mimics the images' intrusiveness.

These apparent flashbacks operate as expressions of trauma, but there is no puzzle to puzzle over. Unlike the puzzle film, which posits an underlying logic, or Chiang's novella, which rigorously alternates between a linear account of

Louise's time with the heptapods and a mostly reverse-order account of Louise's life with Hannah, the flashbacks seem to appear in random order. It is their increasing frequency and clarity—the second series is brighter and ends with diegetic sound (fig. 4.2.2); the third is more focused and even includes dialogue (fig. 4.2.3)—that are notable, as they indicate that the multiple encounters with the heptapods, sleep deprivation, and possibly "radiation poisoning" (Doctor Kettler's hypothesis) are releasing unnegotiated emotions and precipitating a quite comprehensible mental breakdown. The fourth series, depicting Louise at her daughter's side at the hospital, seems to confirm that the linguist is still coping with her loss and is unwilling to confide in others for fear of being dismissed, with Amy Adams's bowed head, closed eyes, tense facial expressions, and trembling hands expressing her character's inner struggle to keep her emotions in check (fig. 4.2.4). The fifth series, which occurs on Louise's final visit to the chamber, revisits the deathbed scenes, but the scene of peaceful communication with the heptapods that frames it suggests that their interaction is helping Louise deal with her trauma rather than perversely exploiting it. On a first viewing, then, Louise's visions are perfectly integrated in a psychological causality established by the prologue, which evokes a subplot of healing through confrontation with the past and with a radically outside force—much like an adult version of *E.T.*, in which a friendly alien heals a broken family.[17]

If, in retrospect, the first clue that these apparent flashbacks could be flash-forwards occurs in the third series when Hannah shows her drawing depicting Mommy and Daddy talking to animals (fig. 4.3.1), on a first viewing the revelation occurs much later, at the dawn of the fourth act, when two

Figures 4.2.1–4.2.4. Flashes of Louise's life with Hannah erupt halfway through the film and gain in visual and aural clarity, leading first-time viewers to deduce that these images of (presumably) the past are getting stronger, and thus that the protagonist is breaking down emotionally and psychologically.

series of mental images end up connecting like pieces of a puzzle. In the first, Hannah asks her mother for the "technical term for when we make a deal"; Louise is at a loss and replies, "If you want science, call your father." The second series is directly triggered by Ian's advising that the military propose a "trade" with the heptapods, which he describes as a "non-zero-sum game"; Louise is suddenly overtaken by images that constitute the sequel to the earlier scene and depict her providing her daughter with the correct answer, the "non-zero-sum game." This is the first time a link is established between Louise's present situation and her visions, but at this stage, the causality lies exclusively in Ian's present comment acting as a memorial trigger; although a male scientist does seem to provide the answer to Hannah's question, the actual connection could still be random. It is ultimately confirmed when Louise penetrates the Shell: the visions show Hannah/the "child" with her drawing and then re-creating her parents' encounter with the heptapods using Play-Doh, and Costello confirms that "Louise sees future" (figs. 4.3.1–4.3.2). As in the season 3 finale of *Lost* (ABC, 2004–2010), the flashbacks have been redefined as flash-forwards, so that the penultimate flashes of Louise and Hannah's conversation on the beach quickly stabilize in a classical mise-en-scène (master shot followed by shot/reverse shots).

On the face of it, the dramatic reversal is quite simple: the opening flashback was actually a flash-forward; Louise was/is haunted by the future, not the past; and the distraught expression worn by Amy Adams in the remembrance scenes expressed not her character's bereavement but puzzlement. In these moments, we had unwittingly been cut off from the protagonist emotionally and cognitively, and what we believed to

Figures 4.3.1–4.3.2. The flash-forward depicting the child's Play-Doh re-creation of her parents' encounters with the heptapods is confirmed as such when Costello reveals that "Louise sees future."

have been internal focalization was actually external focalization. The reveal thus modifies our frame of reference (notably, as provided by the prologue) and reconfigures our spectatorial position, bridging a heretofore unsuspected gap and (re)aligning us with Louise[18]—we are now puzzling over the meaning of these images, as she had been all along. On a meta-level, as Sarah Hatchuel suggests, we are invited to rewatch the story of Louise and Hannah's life, whose pieces the protagonist herself watches anew.[19]

But like many time-travel narratives, *Arrival*'s twist relies on a supplementary paradox, as the film's second and definitive climax, Louise's meeting with General Shang, demonstrates. Louise and the audience now know that her visions show the future, and that her foresight is key to resolving the geopolitical crisis. The paradox is produced by a fairly typical time loop: the future General Shang provides her with his phone number so she can call him from the Montana base and convince him to call off the attack. As Elsaesser notes, a "media-object"—the phone—"is used to build this bridge that forms the loop that transfers knowledge and agency from the person in the future to the person in the past."[20] The device's role in establishing a causal and communicative link between two moments in time had been foreshadowed by the "non-zero-sum game" scenes when Louise invited Hannah to "call" her father. But what Louise's post–alien crisis meeting with the Chinese general also reveals is that the future Louise does not remember everything about the past, not even a momentous event such as saving the world. "Your private number. . . . General, I don't know your private number," Louise says, her hesitation and shaking head expressing perplexity as always. If this second climax provides dramatic resolution, it also reveals that images of the future are just as precarious as images of the past and, thus, that Louise's newfound, nonlinear relation to time is by no means equivalent to omniscience. The time loop not only clarifies but complexifies the portrayal of Louise's post-heptapod subjectivity: she experiences past, present, and future as equally precarious. Paradoxically, then, the real mind game constituted by *Arrival* emerges in the end and invites us to reengage with the film as a puzzle whose pieces may very well not fit.

CRYSTAL-IMAGE AND SUBJECTIVITY

The collapsing of flashback and flash-forward, past, present, and future, brings to mind Gilles Deleuze's "crystal-image," a specific kind of time-image characterized by "the coalescence of an actual image and *its* virtual image, the indiscernibility of two distinct images."[21] The crystal-image is the paradigmatic form of time-image cinema's "crystalline regime," because it encapsulates Henri Bergson's contention that our relation to time is distinguished by "the continual duplication of [one's] present into perception and recollection."[22] *Arrival* does not, however, bear the habitual signs of the crystal-image identified by Deleuze, such as mirrors or actors playing the same or several roles (as in *The Lady from Shanghai* [1947], *That Obscure Object of Desire* [1977], and *Mulholland Dr.*),[23] but some motifs do constitute "mirror-images."[24] Especially prominent are the variety of compositions that express Louise's physical and mental connection to the heptapods through symmetry (Louise's hand and a heptapod tentacle on the windowpane [fig. 3.3.2]; Louise framed by the heptapods in the background; visual echoes (Louise observing a shape in the blurry background) whose movements recall the heptapods' [fig. 4.2.1]); and overlapping shapes within the frames (Louise's head blotting out and seemingly engulfing the Shell in the background [fig. 4.2.4]). In the Shell scenes in particular, the general sense of indiscernibility is enhanced by the soundtrack, the heptapods' voices recalling not only the "'braaams' of *Inception*," "a sound between music and effects,"[25] but the nondiegetic low-frequency blaring notes that evoke the Shell's breadth.

The emergence of the "crystalline regime" is concomitant with the discovery that *Arrival* is a mind-game film. This is not to say that all mind-game films are crystal-images. Deleuze calls "recollection-images" those images that can ultimately be explicated by "psychological causality."[26] Thus, *Mirror* (Tarkovsky, 1975) is crystal-image,[27] *Memento* recollection-image, because the layers of time depicted in Tarkovsky's film cannot be easily assembled in a cause-effect narrative the way those in Nolan's can (and are, in fact, on one of the DVD extras). Inscribed in what appears to be a causal logic, *Arrival*'s flashbacks initially seem to be such recollection-images, operating according to the "organic" regime of movement-image cinema based on the "causal and logical connections" dictated by sensorimotor organization.[28] It is only on a second viewing that *Arrival* can fully be experienced as a crystal-image when we become aware of the flashes' ambiguous status. Ironically, Louise, who perceives them not as memories but as mysteries, recognizes them as eminently contingent and thus responds in a manner that is more in tune with the crystalline regime we experience on a second viewing. In this respect, the prologue is just as instrumental in reframing *Arrival* as crystal-image as it was in setting up a causality-based flashback structure on the first viewing. Indeed, on a first viewing, the use of the adverb "now" in the closing line of Louise's voice-over—"But now I'm not so sure I believe in beginnings and endings"—clearly grounds narrating time in a present that corresponds to a later point in time than the images shown; on a second viewing, however, narrating time becomes quite uncertain given the reconfiguration of Louise's perception following acquisition of Heptapod B. If the instability of the adverb contrasts with the US military's usage of the same word, it finds an echo in General Shang's lines when he gives Louise his personal phone number in the film's climactic flash-forwards, an exchange that is, significantly, framed by his use of the word "now": "Now, eighteen months ago, you did something remarkable. . . . Now you know." Crystalline, the time loop constitutes "a small internal circuit between a present and *its* own past"[29]—"now" and "eighteen months ago"—verbally expressed by the repetition of the word "now." The prologue not only warned us not to trust the ending of the film any more than the beginning; it affirmed the ambiguity of the crystal-image, in which beginnings and endings (the plural is essential in instilling doubt) are mirror images.

The crystalline regime could seem inherent to heptapod language and culture. "Like their ship or their bodies," Dr. Donnelly informs us during the documentary sequence, "their written language has no forward or backward direction." The heptapods, their hieroglyphs, and the Shell (Deleuze identifies the ship as a potential crystal-image because a part of it is concealed under water,[30] while, in this case, it is mainly the Shell's interior that remains opaque) would thus qualify as crystal-images. Their "non-linear" relation to time recalls what Gilles Deleuze and Félix Guattari call a "plane of immanence," that is, a plane that excludes transcendence and in which antithetical terms coexist on the same level.[31] Abbott's death is a neat illustration of this: in nonlinear time, it coexists alongside his life, just as the heptapods' arrival coexists with their need for humanity's help "in three thousand years," a point Costello significantly reveals to Louise after informing her of Abbott's passing. It would be tempting to conclude that movement-image cinema would be on the side of the human, time-image cinema on the side of the heptapod, but putting forward such a dichotomy would be a gross misunderstanding of both Deleuze and *Arrival*.

First, for Deleuze, the crystalline regime of time-image cinema is eminently human insofar as it is an expression of our experience of life. "The only subjectivity is time," Deleuze says, adapting Bergson, "non-chronological time grasped in its foundation, and it is we who are internal to time, not the other way round."[32] Again, *Mirror* is a paradigmatic example of a film whose temporal complexity is by no means fantastic and can entirely be put down to the functioning of human memory. (This should come as no surprise given Tarkovsky's belief that "time and memory merge into each other; they are like the two sides of a medal,"[33] which resonates with Bergson's philosophy, just as the Russian director's assertion that cinema "conveys awareness of facts and aesthetic structures existing and changing within time" resonates with Deleuze's descriptions of the pure optical and sound image.[34]) Second, within the diegesis of *Arrival*, the heptapod worldview and language are very much founded on causality, albeit an alien one: in other/heptapod words, there is no hesitation between the actual image and its virtual image, of past, present, and future, because they coexist and make sense at the same time. Thus, *Arrival* qualifies as crystal-image only if it is understood as an expression of Louise Banks's subjectivity, a subjectivity that is characterized as being potentially affected by the heptapod worldview from the start, and whose potential causality is lost on us or, at the least, remains fragmentary, as it does so for Louise herself, whose realization that she "can read" Heptapod B is expressed by intercutting flashes early on. The hesitation between the actual image and its virtual image overlaps not so much with the question of chronological time as such (past, present, and future) as with that of subjective experience (time but also space experienced by human or heptapod). It is Louise Banks's liminal status between human and heptapod that makes her—more than the heptapods—an embodiment of the crystal-image, and the film in its entirety an expression of her subjectivity disseminating its many reflections. Significantly, Louise's realization about her understanding of Heptapod B is prompted by a flash in which she explains to her daughter that her name, Hannah, is a "palindrome," or a word that "reads the same forward—and backward," and that constitutes yet another crystal-image. Psychological/narrative causality is thus subordinated to a crystal-image, and movement-image cinema (the heroine's saving the day) is embedded in time-image cinema (her subjective experience).

The science fiction action movie tropes, structured within the diegesis through the presence of the military and the media, are initially associated with movement-image cinema and, on a first viewing, serve to conceal and restrain the crystal-image. But they are ultimately revealed to be reflections contained within the crystalline structure made manifest by the mirror prologue and epilogue. This is evinced by the final sequence of media images. Unlike earlier sequences, the TV screen does not fill up the frame but appears in a black void (fig. 4.4.1); other screens begin to appear and recede into the background, until the frame is filled with a mosaic of semitransparent screens like Photoshop layers (fig. 4.4.2). The screens, unlike the film's many others, are not placed in diegetic locales but appear in a virtual space with no justification whatsoever. Coming at the end of the film, this sequence could be just another one of Louise's visions expressed in the crystalline regime. It also recalls another variety of time-image, which Deleuze calls "the simultaneity of points of present, these points breaking with all external succession, and carrying out quantic jumps between the presents which are doubled by the past, the future and the present itself."[35] In effect, the multiple screens, on which various anchorpeople converse in different languages about different events, tend to virtualize the experience of the actual, to turn it into a multiplicity of presents competing against each other for relevance. What the sequence does, however, is reveal that this quality of the contemporary mediascape preexists the heptapod arrival and Louise's new mindset. It is not, for that matter, limited to the news media but also includes the screens the military and scientists rely on to communicate with each other. The presence of Agent Halpern in front of these screens points to the subject's—and the spectator's—own relation to these multitudes of presents. While individually each screen constitutes an instance of Baudrillardian simulation, as an ensemble they constitute not just the hyperreal, "the generation of models of a real without origin or reality," but a multitude of "hyperreal events, no longer with a specific content or end, but indefinitely refracted by each other."[36]

Surprisingly, then, time-image cinema emerges, here, from the accumulation of the very clichés it meant to destroy—Deleuze identifies the "crisis of movement-image" as originating in a desire to "escape from a world of clichés," as "tearing a real image from" the clichés imposed by "sensory-motor linkages."[37] We thus see how profoundly reliant on modernism Deleuze's theory of time-image cinema was in the first place, and how it can be rethought from a postmodernist perspective. Time-image is a quality of both modernist (Louise's

Figures 4.4.1–4.4.2. The final news media sequence: a TV screen materializes in an unidentified black space, then proceeds to recede into the background, as other TV screens appear and follow suit, an image that seems to reveal the crystalline quality of the Baudrillardian hyperreal.

moderately Bergsonian/Deleuzian/Tarkovskian experience of the world) and postmodernist (the constant and multiple mediatizations of the real) fragmentation. If *Arrival* unwittingly reveals this potential, it nonetheless works to contain postmodernist fragmentation (the points of present associated with the media) within modernist subjectivity (the hesitation concerning Louise's point of view). In effect, it is further tempered by the handling of the soundtrack in this final news media sequence. Not only does the voice remain the principal means of communication and affirm its privileged position on the soundtrack, but the narration selects specific voices to avoid cacophony and hierarchize the information being delivered and the languages and cultures being foregrounded, thus yielding to the norms of classical narration. The soundtrack plays this unifying role more generally throughout the film; as James Buhler has noted, the sounds associated with both the logograms and the flashes "are anchored to particular temporal moments and serve to distinguish the temporal layers and secure their integrity even as they offer passage to the new temporal layer."[38] The concluding media sequence is thus paradigmatic of how *Arrival* performs a balancing act between time-image and movement-image cinema, modernism and postmodernism, aesthetics and politics, and art and blockbuster cinema.

The question of time is not limited just to the temporality of an alien language or culture. Dramatic tension is produced by the conflicting relations to time nurtured by the human parties dealing with the crisis. By siding with duration and reflection (slow science) against urgency and economy (the media and the military), *Arrival* positions itself a few degrees closer to art cinema than to mainstream blockbuster, while exploiting the latter's energy to its advantage, if only to maintain interest in its hard soft science fiction project. It likewise exploits the mind-game film trend as a plot twist and an invitation for repeated viewings, while insisting on the precariousness of its puzzle pieces (Louise Banks's memories of the present, future, and past). While Elsaesser's argument (as paraphrased by Warren Buckland) that the mind-game film's "'work[ing] through' paradoxes of representation and paradoxes of time" potentially offers a "critique of Western notions of knowledge and representation" is doubtful given how US/Euro-centric the majority of these films are,[39] the statement resonates in part with *Arrival*'s proposal to offer a glimpse of an alien relation to time characterized by immanence that is not entirely devoid of causality. Louise's human-heptapod—and thus eminently posthuman—subjectivity is expressed through an aesthetics of time that, in many ways, resembles the crystalline regime of time-image cinema, although the film's imagining the possibility of a cliché-laden hyperreal time-image does pose a conundrum for Deleuzian theory and invites us to rethink time-image cinema in the age of postmodern globalization. At heart, the 2016 film is a bit closer to *Mirror* than *Memento*, and perhaps takes its cue, in this regard, from *Solaris*, a film that is similarly bookended by images of a family house in a countryside environment emphasizing the elements (sky, water, woods). In combining the cognitive activity of the mind-game film with the sensitive experience of time-image cinema, *Arrival* is a many-layered gift for all viewers. Like *Mulholland Dr.*,[40] it ultimately favors the sensitive experience by emphasizing the protagonist's physical and emotional voyage more than her intellectual enterprise, and it encourages us to sense rather than make sense of it all.

Arrival as an Experience of Space

HOUSE, CAMP, SHELL

Referring with its title not only to a moment but to an event that took place somewhere, *Arrival* is just as much about space as it is about time. Space, place, and landscape, though related terms, are by no means synonymous. Geographer Yi-Fu Tuan, for instance, defines place contra space: a place has coordinates and boundaries (it is "closed" and marks a "pause"); place is associated with stasis, whereas space is a more abstract concept evoking a dynamic expanse (space entails "movement").[1] Film scholar André Gardies makes a similar distinction when he describes space as "general, latent, virtual" and place as "particular" and "identifiable";[2] by arguing that places and landscapes "actualize" space,[3] he suggests that space is their condition of emergence. For Martin Lefebvre, in a work of art or fiction at least, a place remains countable (it can be broken down into "segments") and identifiable as a "setting" even when it is unnamed and indeterminate; landscape, on the other hand, is a sort of "anti-setting" that emerges when a film emphasizes an outside space's singular value rather than its narrative action.[4] Thus, a place can be pinpointed, a landscape framed, while space is an unbounded expanse. *Arrival*, we shall see, offers an exploration that takes us from the boundaries of place and the conventions of the landscape tradition to the expanses of cinematic space.

Arrival is characterized by its small number of locales. The vast majority of the story takes place at the Montana site, a mountain meadow, either at the military camp or at the foot of or within the nearby Shell, and the action is relayed by the human characters' moving back and forth between the two. Dramatically speaking, the film is thus characterized by its unity of space, which reinforces the screenwriter's reduction of Chiang's story's time setting. The third main locale, Louise's house, contrasts sharply with the Montana setting: first, as a private and domestic space located in the woods next to a body of water; second, because of its structural role, as both a frame for the narrative and, in the third act, a disruptive element. The film's other places include the hospital, the university where Louise works, the reception hall where she meets General Shang, and the Shell sites worldwide, which are depicted in the media footage until the aliens' final departure. The hospital, present only in the prologue, is the second space shared by Louise and Hannah, and represents a desolate offshoot of the house. The university and the reception hall buttress the narrative frame provided by the prologue and epilogue. Bookending the film, they not only mark the beginning and end of the alien invasion plot but mirror each other, as each is the stage of a meeting between Louise and a member of the military who pulls out a communication device (Weber the digital recorder, Shang the phone); the difference in the narrative function is reinforced by the play on degrees of occupation of space (students and personnel are deserting the university [fig. 5.6.2], while the reception hall is crowded).

Louise's house is presented as an isolated place, in the woods looking out onto a substantial body of water. It is built from the elemental materials that surround it: stone (the side walls) and wood (the roof, living room floor, and ceiling). In spite of its French windows on either side of a spacious living room (fig. 4.1.2) and the broad windows in Louise's bedroom, the house is plunged in relative darkness, bathed in the gray light seeping in from outside because its inhabitant employs no artificial lighting apart from the television screens. It is a melancholy place, inhabited by the specter of Louise's loss, a mood the prologue's soundtrack immediately instills through Amy Adams's mournful voice-over and the B-flat minor harmony of Max Richter's "On the Nature of Daylight." Significantly, the house is much brighter when inhabited by precancer Hannah's joyful presence, most scenes taking place either outside, suffused in bright sunlight, or at the child's bedside, bathed in a warm orange artificial light; the silver backlight creeps in only when Hannah tells her mother she hates her. In the prologue and epilogue, Louise's house is clearly an instance of pathetic fallacy; it reflects a mood that she fails to ward off and maybe even nurtures, and that is thus based on a metonymic relationship between house and inhabitant. The intrusion of these images of the house in the third act, as Simon Bréan has noted, replays the prologue's chromatic and emotional shift[5]—from colorful brightness to a monochromatic orange brown—but the sunlit lakeside images inspire a different interpretation on a second viewing, when we understand that the bright exteriors provide no indication of Louise's mood and mindset while in Montana; significantly, the dark interiors of Louise's house in the "non-zero-sum game" scenes reflect the narration's emotional and subjective realignment with the heroine and thus the return of pathetic fallacy.

In many respects, the Montana military camp is the exact opposite of Louise's house and is more of a variation on another workplace: her university. It is a temporary place whose walls are made of artificial fabrics held up by poles, which at the end of the movie can be "evacuated within the hour." It is also a closed space dominated by artificial light, silver in the work rooms, yellowish brown in the corridors and sleeping quarters—military tents often have windows, so the lack of windows opening onto the outside is a staging decision that may be justified diegetically by the fear of contamination but that, dramatically at least, contributes to the sense of being cut off not only from the rest of the world but even from their immediate environment (the Shell and mountain prairie are not visible from inside). The camp is immediately presented as dynamic, bustling with people, activity, movement, and noises. Accordingly, it is introduced in a helicopter shot that circles over the base while registering the swooshing of the blades (fig. 5.1.1); the high-angle establishing shot reveals a central base made up of tents, with a few mobile homes on one side and vehicles and soldiers moving about. The sense of movement is immediately confirmed when Ian and Louise, upon landing, walk across the camp, accompanied by eye-level handheld tracking shots revealing soldiers carrying a gurney or pitching tents, and helicopters landing in the background.

The camp is just as dynamic indoors, a state that is again expressed through noises (voices but also the outside sounds that penetrate the less-than-soundproof tents) and camera movement. Track-ins and -outs follow Louise and Ian as they are led into a variety of rooms: Medical, a work room occupied exclusively by soldiers, the video conference room, Ian's team's room, Louise's team's room (fig. 5.1.2), the decontamination room. Later scenes introduce other rooms: the monitoring room, the phone call room, the mobile home in which Louise sleeps, the meeting room. Clearly, the military base's topography is determined by functionality, including providing a degree of group or individual privacy (Medical, the decontamination and meeting rooms, the sleeping quarters). Each workstation is characterized by a certain area of expertise and, consequently, led by the appropriate person (Dr. Kettler in Medical, Agent Halpern in the video conference room, Ian in the physics room, Louise in the linguistics room), evincing a definite hierarchy (Weber, who leads the tour, functions, in this respect, as a link between the rooms). The workstations are not messy but filled with necessary equipment (tables, screens, phones). The camp's openness is equally functional—there are doors and windows between the workstations—and ensures the speedy communication of relevant information from one person/team/room to another. By and large, the dramatic and symbolic treatment of space overlaps with, and is justified by, the military camp's functionality. This is especially apparent in the final scene, in which Louise seeks the only closed room—the decontamination cell—that will allow her to conclude her phone conversation with General Shang. Indeed, the cell provides not only protection; it is a liminal place, with doors on either side, that acts as a filter between inside and outside, Shell and base, skin and hazmat suit. This very practical in-betweenness makes it the most appropriate setting for the time-loop sequence connecting present and future, while also playing on the conventional sci-fi horror inversion whereby the danger no longer comes from without but from within, when the soldiers end up aiming their rifles at the scientist who was meant to at least contribute to saving the day (fig. 5.1.3).

Devoid of apparent windows and doors, the Shell seems to present an organic wholeness, one capable of unproblematically integrating contrasts such as its outer smoothness and the irregular surface of its inner walls. Resembling a floating egg-shaped stone, it is a mineral space, as will be confirmed by the texture of its inner walls. Its organic, geometric, and topographic simplicity is set against the military camp's complexity, its blankness without and emptiness within against the military hustle and bustle. And yet, in many ways, the Shell is the minimalist version of the military camp, and Louise and Ian, led by Weber, walk us through it just as they did the camp. Composed of one straight corridor (the antechamber), one rectangular meeting room (the chamber), and finally one undetermined and possibly more intimate space (the gaseous environment inhabited by the heptapods), the Shell is hyperfunctional, and its hyperfunctionality testifies to the heptapods' technological superiority, as does its smooth surface,[6] much like another benevolent alien's (Klaatu's) UFO in *The Day the Earth Stood Still*. The chamber is also presented as the minimalist version of Louise's living room, a similarity the establishing shot of the chamber that tilts up from the ceiling draws attention to.

Though highly generic, the three main locales do not correspond to Marc Augé's definition of a "non-place," "a space which cannot be defined as relational, or historical, or concerned with identity,"[7] because, as Sophie Mayer notes, they offer interaction, not self-centered anonymity.[8] Their function

Figures 5.1.1–5.1.3. The base camp, a highly ordered and functional place with rooms devoted to specific teams and tasks, also harbors a liminal space, the decontamination room, an ideal setting for a time loop and an act of resistance.

is narrative, emotional, and thematic: they are stages; they operate as instances of pathetic fallacy, expressing Louise's emotions; and they evoke, because of their respective materials, different relations to temporality, from the highly (the tents) to moderately (Louise's wooden house) ephemeral to the quasi-eternal (the mineral Shell and mountain prairie). This is also true of the hospital, where the waiting room's geometrical irregularity reflects the life-shattering diagnosis, the corridor's circularity (fig. 5.6.1) the cycle of grief and (on a second viewing) Louise's nonlinear relation to time. In spite of their physical differences, these locales share some common traits (functionality, intimacy) and social and aesthetic functions (interaction, pathetic fallacy)—most poignantly, a common color scheme dominated by a silvery-gray hue: it is the color of sorrow, of Hannah's hospital, spilling onto the rest of the film, much like the clouds over the Montana mountains. As the second viewing will prove, these locales are, in effect, Louise's mental spaces. Time and space, as the title announced, are by no means separate but form a continuum.

MUNDANE SPACE, SUBLIME SPACE

Though *Arrival* is a first-contact movie set exclusively on Earth, it differs from traditional alien invasion movies, and even from predecessors like *Close Encounters of the First Kind* and *Contact*, insofar as it features several key scenes inside the aliens' spacecraft early on. If on the outside the Shell conforms to the science fiction movie cliché of the "'rationally' sleek" spaceship,[9] on the inside it is an organic space, lined with mineral walls, filled with mist, and devoid of apparent technological devices—its communication, aeronautic, and energy technologies are undetectable to human beings, Ian explains in the documentary sequence. With its potentially noxious air (hence the hazmat suits), it is an alien environment contained within a spaceship—and thus a synecdoche of an alien planet, just like human spaceships in many science fiction works are often organized as mini-Earths or Noah's Arks (*Silent Running*, the original *Battlestar Gallactica*, *Elysium* [2013]). Hovering above the Earth, the Shell has its own physical laws that defy the force of gravity; entering it requires jumping through a zero-gravity field before landing on the antechamber's wall at a 90-degree angle. The alien space is thus characterized by its topsy-turviness, a quality that is illustrated when the images start spinning on a soldier's wrist monitor and expressed through camerawork when the camera slowly revolves counterclockwise to capture Marks's leap into the antechamber,[10] frames Marks and his colleague upside down with the lift in the bottom of the frame, zooms in/tracks out *Vertigo*-style on Ian facing the void, and later tilts up from the floor to reveal the humans walking upside down, and thus that the floor was actually a ceiling. The topsy-turviness not only foreshadows the heptapods' unique relation to time but suggests that it is more generally their relation to space-time that differs from the humans'.

The first Shell visit scene portrays the exploration of an alien environment in a similar fashion as astronauts reconnoitering a planet in the *Star Trek* and *Alien* franchises. It is a frontier space, as Gervais notes, or space exploration on Earth, as Guilhem Billaudel pointed out to me when justifying the inclusion of *Arrival* in his corpus of 2010s space movies. The military and scientists are suited up, transported to a scissor lift that raises them vertically through the Shell door, and subjected to a decontamination process upon their return. The Montana site functions like a slice of outer space, the military camp like a human spaceship stationed on or orbiting around the moon-like Shell, and the lift, with its familiar construction work beeps, like a rocket or teletransportation device. The narration alternates between wider shots that position the humans in space, and close-ups and medium close-ups of Louise and Ian that register their emotions; camera movements are slow, the tilts and pans evoking the lightness of zero gravity, the tracking shots matching the pace at which the hazmat suits allow the humans to advance. The various components of the soundtrack reinforce the impression that this is actually a scene of planetary or spatial exploration: the radio voices and their lingo evoke take-off and landing sequences or moments when explorers communicate with their ship or base; the whale call–like F-G motif resembles a fragment of a wavering melody such as those that we have come to associate with space since Bernard Hermann's score for *The Day the Earth Stood Still* or Alexander Courage's *Star Trek* theme—composed of three half-notes and a half-sigh, the plucked-string theme in the title "First Encounter" mimics the humans' slow steps and echoes their and our sense of anticipation of what lies at the end of the antechamber.

With its darkness, cavernous walls, and Lovecraftian creatures semi-concealed in mist, the inside of the Shell is also an eminently Gothic space, as if the humans were prospecting the depths of a planet or an ocean (hence Weber's asking Amy whether she had "scuba-dive[d] before"). It is, however, utterly devoid of labyrinthine twists and turns or nooks and crannies, which are conducive to getting lost and/or surprised by dangerous creatures. So while it mobilizes many of the recognizable sci-fi horror tropes of planetary exploration, Louise and Ian's first visit nonetheless resembles a minimalist, mundane, and relatively anticlimactic take on the *Nostromo* and *Prometheus* crews' exploration of LV-426 and LV-223 in Ridley Scott's 1979 and 2012 films.

Like *Close Encounters of the Third Kind*, however, *Arrival* very much emphasizes the sublime quality of the UFO and its inhabitants, as Vincent Jaunas has noted.[11] Famously described by Edmund Burke as a combination of "astonishment" and "terror" that could be provoked, among other things, by "obscurity," "vacuity," or "vastness,"[12] the sublime is a quality traditionally associated not only with the Gothic but also with science fiction;[13] Sobchack insists, notably, on the emotions the special effects in movies like *Close Encounters of the Third Kind* are geared to produce.[14] But I would argue that the sublime is not a mere matter of a special effects bonanza entirely disconnected from the rest of the material; the spectacle remains an eminently spatial one and retains a link to the Gothic. *Arrival*'s poetics thus highlight the Shell's grandeur, and the awe and terror it inspires: tilts up and down the surface of the Shell emphasizing its size and the humans' puniness, and its potential to obliterate the space of the frame with its darkness (fig. 5.2.3), are regularly synched with blaring held notes that evoke its physical proportions (because of their length and guttural texture) and the emotion it provokes (because of their volume and low frequencies); track-ins and -outs evoke not only distance but the Shell's force of attraction, reflecting the combination of fear and curiosity about what lies at the end of the tunnel. Special effect, sound effect, and spatial effect thus collaborate in the sublime aesthetics, and the special effect remains spatial to its core.

This is evinced at the end of the movie, when the other Shell sites are finally shown without being mediated by television screens. Indebted as much to the Devils Tower scenes of *Close Encounters of the Third Kind* as to *2001*'s famous *Blue Danube Waltz* sequence, the final departure montage sequence emphasizes massiveness but also grace as the editing orchestrates a choreography of movement—the Shanghai Shell rising to the right, the Siberian Shell to the left, the Greenland Shell to the right, the Indian Ocean Shell in the center. The sense of unison is reinforced by slow camera movements (mostly tilt-ups), the silver-gray color palette as they vanish within a silver smoke that very much resembles the heptapods' gaseous habitat, and the enveloping soundscape, with two cuts synched to the D-sharp to A-sharp motif. Sublime landscapes and even cityscapes are the apt sites of sublime events because the supernatural event merely makes manifest the "awe and solemnity of the divine presence" such environments already evoke.[15] Contrary to what Sobchack suggests, the sublime in science fiction cinema derives not so much from the virtuoso special effects and cinematography themselves, but from how they give form to the object's or landscape's sublime potential.

In effect, the Shells reconfigure the traditional landscape, revealing its plasticity, its capacity to welcome an alien shape. On Louise's and our first glimpse of the Shell, the massive vessel dominates the Montana landscape (fig. 5.2.1). Positioned according to the classical rule of thirds, it integrates the composition harmoniously, all the while forcefully reconfiguring the landscape: its backlit darkness contrasts with the whiteness of the clouds, its smooth surface with the textures of the clouds, mountain peaks, and prairie below; its imposing verticality makes the landscape appear predominantly horizontal in

Figures 5.2.1–5.2.3. The Montana Shell is first revealed in a landscape shot, which the aerial track-in steers away from before the spaceship completely obliterates the frame, but the Shell will nonetheless remain a daunting background presence throughout the film. Its sublime potential is highlighted by allowing it to threateningly obliterate the frame (on the first visit) or harmoniously integrate into the landscape (at the end when they depart).

spite of the mountains; its summit touching the upper frame points to its connection with outer space. The egg-like Shell resembles a nascent outgrowth in the environment, but it is also a presence surveilling it, thus blurring the distinction between shape and figure, and between landscape and portrait. As the helicopter shot tracks in, the Shell increasingly takes up more room in the composition, eventually occupying the center before the shot circles around the military camp. And yet, even relegated offscreen, the Shell remains a daunting presence—we anticipate the helicopter will pivot 360 degrees so we can see it again, but we have to wait for the next shot in the next scene, when Louise cannot resist the urge to look over her left shoulder in its direction (fig. 5.2.2). The reconfiguration of the cinematic landscape is an effect of both composition and camera movement. Nicolas Bolduc, Deakins, and Villeneuve resort to similar aerial shots to highlight and alter the geometrical coordinates of Toronto in *Enemy*; Ciudad Juárez in *Sicario*; the Central Valley, Los Angeles, and Las Vegas in *Blade Runner 2049*;[16] and Arrakeen and the sandy environment of Arrakis in *Dune*. This reconfiguration is a promise of the exploration of cinematic space that will mainly take place indoors.

EXPLORING THE PROPERTIES OF CINEMATIC SPACE

The Shell chamber is not just an allegorical movie theater; it is literally a movie set, on which military personnel document the scientists' interactions with the heptapods. With just one camera fixed on a tripod, the military's functional, one-track approach to recording the encounters sharply contrasts with the wide array of shot angles and sizes, compositions, and editing techniques that make up the film's narration, and whose variety the reframed images of the same shot on the monitoring room screens cannot compete with.[17] In effect, the chamber's characteristics—spaciousness and emptiness, its rectangular shape and textured walls—are favorable for the exploration of the plastic quality of cinematic space. Cinematic space encompasses but is not limited to the places and spaces represented in films (cities, natural environments, etc.) or the pictorial genre that is the landscape; and while such concerns, as well as the construction of narrative and dramatic space, have received much critical attention,[18] the plastic qualities of cinematic space have often been overlooked.[19] Antoine Gaudin defines cinematic space as a three-pronged "stake": it is "a *given* of the representation" (space is a component of the world that is filmed, whether or not it is fictional), "an aesthetic and dramatic *problem*" (not only is space organized in a specific way to please the eye, produce emotion, be comprehensive, and contribute to the narrative, but it can be the very subject of the film), and a "semi-empirical, semi-imaginary *construction*"[20] (cinematic space is on the screen but also extends beyond it; it is a "quality" in the Deleuzian sense,[21] something to be experienced from a phenomenological perspective). Cinematic space thus exists in a dialogical relationship with its raw material, concrete space, whose properties it can tone up or down, but which, reciprocally, plays up or down the properties of film image and sound. The Shell's cavernous chamber provides just the place for the investigation of these properties.

The heptapod encounter scenes are characterized by a general series of features that constitute a compositional system and thus a poetics.[22] Deep-focus compositions emphasize the chamber's spaciousness and emptiness, and frontal, back, and lateral angles its rectangular shape. Frontal shots of the screen tend to insist on its flatness (fig. 3.1.1), reverse shots of the humans on the chamber's breadth and depth (fig. 3.2.1). Three-quarter angles reconfigure cinematic space, creating oblique lines out of perpendicular ones and irregular quadrilaterals (fig. 5.4.1). Compositions resorting to salient angles (high, low, three-quarter) tend to accommodate more room for the chamber's walls, thus foregrounding their mineral texture and contrasting it with the gaseous material swirling beyond the chamber's window (fig. 5.4.2). Diegetic space can also be filtered through profilmic elements such as the hazmat suit's translucent mask (fig. 3.2.3), which tends to flatten cinematic space. In sound film, cinematic space is equally an aural phenomenon. The chamber is characterized by a tangible reverb with a one-echo delay. Its soundscape comprises the low and infralow frequencies of sounds emitted by the heptapods' voices and movements; the medium frequencies of the humans' breaths and voices, which are higher when distorted by their mikes and headphones; and the high frequencies of the canary's chirping. The chamber's properties are brought out by the presence of the human characters. Their suits' orange fabric and their delicate skin contrast with the dark minerality of the walls and the bright, swirling fog. The human figures' puniness endows the very long shot compositions with a sense of scale (fig. 3.3.1), while in the full, medium, and close shots of the screen, they do not compromise but enhance the sense of flatness like neat cutouts, a welcome effect of the green screen technique. The variety of shots and compositions emphasizes oppositions of color, texture, lines, and shapes in order to express the impassable rift between alien and human, materialized by the window. But the visiting scenes also reveal the vitality of cinematic space in the dynamic orchestration of compositions.

On Louise and Ian's first visit, the scene's overall treatment of cinematic space shifts from depth to flatness while mostly retaining a sense of frontality and rectangularity. With the exception of one medium close-up of Louise, the walk down the antechamber is narrated in two deep-focus very long shots that emphasize the immense distance the characters have to traverse. The frontality of the compositions creates vanishing points that overlap either with the door or the chamber at either end of the tunnel, indicating the points of departure and arrival while instilling a sense of vertigo, since we know from the Shell's design that the tunnel is at a 90-degree angle with the Earth below. The 180-degree shot/reverse shot of the antechamber emphasizes its length and claustrophobic quality (neither side provides respite), evoking the pressure exerted by the walls and the mysterious space on the human figures while materializing its paradoxical airiness; the light from the flashlights and the window beyond not only highlights the walls' texture but also gives presence to the spaciousness instead of creating a pitch-black environment. Reinforcing the sense of verticality, the track-out and track-in express both the distance the characters have to cover and our dread of watching them fall down the hole or of being sucked down into the image ourselves. These emotions are conveyed by the music, the plucked string evoking danger, the blaring held notes the physical distance and potential fall. We are contemplating and experiencing a void, a potential vacuum, in which whiteness is, as in Edgar Allan Poe's *Adventures of Arthur Gordon Pym* and Lovecraft's *At the Mountains of Madness*, paradoxically more threatening than the quasi-all-encompassing darkness and the unknown space that lies beyond the walls.[23] The tracking shots and deep focus also preclude an aesthetic threat—the flattening of the image—and ensure that the film will not fall into the abstraction of early experimental cinema like Hans Richter's 1921 *Rhythmus 21*.

The chamber itself is first introduced by a deep-focus very long shot when the humans walk in, and shot size subsequently alternates (between very long shots of the chamber and full to close shots of the humans and the bird cage) and eventually diminishes, a tendency that is marked by the use of track-ins (the low-angle three-quarter shot of Marks; the eye-level back shot of Weber, Louise, Ian, and Marks; the frontal shot of the window). The scene's climax—the heptapods' arrival—concludes with close-ups of Ian, Louise, and Weber, and reverse shots of the window in which the frame ultimately vanishes. The sense of flatness, first introduced by the POV shot through Louise's helmet, becomes the dominant visual regime by the end of the scene, when the window fills up the frame and Louise appears engulfed in it; the brief insert of Louise's left hand clenching, with the blurry window and heptapod in the left background, expresses not only the character's fear, much like the earlier insert of the canary, but a visual resistance to the pull of flatness and symmetry, which will later produce images of Louise's hand pressed to the window (fig. 3.3.2). The editing is instrumental in preventing the overall progression from depth to flatness from becoming either too random (and spatially disorienting) or monolithic (and boring). Links between shots with differing compositional features are based on at least one similarity: the humans are depicted entering the chamber upside down in back and lateral shots; frontal compositions edited in shot/

reverse shot connect shallow-focus close-ups and deep-focus very long shots; the track-in is used to connect a series of shots with differing sizes and angles.

On the second visit, compositions are linked according to similar principles, but the main tension in terms of cinematic space is no longer between depth and flatness but between horizontality and verticality on the one hand and obliqueness and circularity on the other. Louise's attempt at communicating with the heptapods visually breaks down the first visit's frontality, an idea immediately encapsulated by the over-the-shoulder-shot of the whiteboard (fig. 5.3.1). The sequence thus alternates between three-quarter angles on the one hand and frontal, back, and lateral angles on the other, and it concludes not on the visual dominance of flatness when the heptapods write on the window—on the contrary, the window frame is reintegrated in the compositions—but on a series of three-quarter close shots of Louise, Ian, and Weber. The three-quarter compositions reconfigure cinematic space, rectangular shapes like the whiteboard (fig. 5.3.1), the window (fig. 5.3.2), and the chamber itself (figs. 3.2.1, 5.4.1) now producing oblique lines that crisscross the composition and sometimes exit the frame along nonparallel lines, inviting our gaze to venture beyond the frame. The visual reconfiguration would mainly seem to be an effect of framing and editing, but the stage design also plays a part; in effect, the chamber walls' irregular textures and the window's rounded corners, which significantly become particularly prominent in the three-quarter shots, accommodate other forms, so that such shots also become an exploration of the chamber's more discrete properties.

Louise uncovers yet another unsuspected property of the chamber—the convex surface of the screen (fig. 3.3.1)—on

Figures 5.3.1–5.3.2. Second visit: three-quarter angles reconfigure cinematic space, horizontal and vertical lines making way for oblique ones and revealing the chamber's less salient irregular properties.

her third visit. The treatment of cinematic space, which is initially similar to the second visit's, is marked by the return of frontality when Louise takes off her suit and walks up to the screen—but with a significant difference: frontality no longer makes manifest a distance but its bridging. If Louise initially appears like a figure engulfed in the screen's vastness, the presence of Ian, who has taken off his helmet but not his suit and thus appears as an orange glob on the bottom right edge of the frame, destabilizes the symmetry and flatness (fig. 5.4.2). Finally, the sense of scale is attenuated by the subsequent close

Figures 5.4.1–5.4.2. Third visit: frontality is reinstated via a high-angle long shot of the humans that could represent the heptapods' perspective, while flatness is produced through a back shot that sets the human figure (Louise) in opposition to the heptapods and an orange blob (Ian).

shots of the humans and heptapods communicating, a situation foreshadowed earlier by the POV shots from both Louise's and the heptapods' perspective (fig. 5.4.1).

Louise's final solitary visit in the Shell is an apt climax, aesthetically speaking, as it proposes to bypass what had, through sheer repetition of the chamber visit scenes, become not only a narrative dead end but an aesthetic one. By taking us beyond the walls and screen, the final visit offers another mode of cinematic space that is the counterpoint to that composed in the chamber scenes—a space that is less shape than texture. The heptapods' actual habitat is revealed to be without ceiling and walls, and the floor on which Louise is standing appears rounded, highly irregular, and, like crystals or bubbles, possibly composed of a solidified version of the ship's atmosphere. Though it resembles an infinite space because the Shell walls remain invisible, it is by no means empty, filled as it is with gaseous matter. The soundtrack endows the matter that had previously been glimpsed through the window with a sense of presence, as the soundscape is now inhabited by higher-pitched noises resembling ghostly voices in addition to the lower wailing notes and tangible reverb that has already characterized the antechamber's and chamber's soundscape. This space does not seem to provide geometric properties the film frame can ideally exploit. The sequence thus describes a shift from a gaseous space with no apparent coordinates to a simulated Euclidean space. As soon as the pod is filled with the gaseous matter, Louise is immediately entangled in the alien environment, her hair rippling under its pressure. Louise's disorientation is expressed through Adams's performance in close-ups, of course, but furthered by a series of three false eyeline matches. Indeed, every time Louise examines her surroundings (looks down, up, or behind), the subsequent reverse shot first reproduces what appears to be the object of her attention (the ice-like floor [fig. 5.5.1], a sound coming from above, an unseen presence [fig. 5.5.2]), before tracking in, tilting down, or panning right to reveal Louise's body within the same shot. Cinematic space is relatively stabilized once Costello enters the picture and an establishing shot positions Louise in relation to the heptapod and the pod that transported her here: two figures and one shape thus inhabit what appears to be an indeterminate space in a state of constant flux (fig. 5.5.3). During Costello and Louise's exchange, the narration then forcefully configures this unstable environment into a comprehensible cinematic space by imposing the familiar properties that characterized the chamber visit scenes: scale and the lack thereof are juxtaposed, with shot/reverse shots alternating between high/low and eye-level angles, while the all-permeating gaseous matter endows this hyper-deep space with a sense of flatness, which allows the hieroglyphs to materialize as if on invisible screens alongside the other shapes and figures.

If the visiting scenes no doubt offer the film's most intense treatment of cinematic space, they constitute just as much a mise en abyme of the film's reception (as explored in chapter 3) as of its creative project. While the dream sequence provides the most obvious example of the contamination of cinematic space effected by the transformation of Louise's relation to space-time, more generally many of the chamber's qualities can be found in all the locales depicted in the opening scenes (Louise's house, the hospital, her university), as is suggested by the fact that Louise's return to Earth is narrated by a shot of her standing in her living room instead of inside the pod. The opening shot (fig. 4.1.1)—a deep-focus long shot that tilts down from the ceiling before tracking in, eye-level, on the windows—brings out not so much the spaciousness of Louise's living room as its geometric complexity: the camera movement follows the lines traced by the ceiling wainscoting, then confronts the symmetric windows with their parallel vertical lines and broken horizontal ones that simultaneously divide the roomscape within and the landscape beyond into a series of fragments, inviting connections between the lines and shapes that make up the various pictures (the telescope and

Figures 5.5.1–5.5.4. Louise's journey inside the heptapod habitat beyond the chamber window: familiar properties (a floor, the positioning of human and alien figures in space) are imposed on a space that destabilizes traditional Euclidean spatial coordinates and accommodates a fluid or gaseous regime.

the tree, the table and the distant shore, the pendant light and the canopy of leaves). The living room is reintroduced later in two slowly tracking-in, deep-focus establishing shots (fig. 4.1.2) that insist, conversely, on its spaciousness and textures, the 180-degree shot/reverse shot materializing the airiness itself, as in the antechamber ascension scene. Two deep-focus long shots that slowly track in emphasize the hospital's gloomy depth and emptiness, while the circular lines of the corridor paradoxically invite our gaze to escape the frame while blocking it with the massive rectangular block created by the convex wall on the right, visually demonstrating that any escape would be illusory, as the corridor would eventually bring us full circle, back to the same exact spot (fig. 5.6.1). The lecture hall scene, like the subsequent communication scenes, is characterized by frontality (with frontal and back shots of Louise and her students) until the siren sounds, heralding a radical shift in shot scale and angle, which emphasizes the room's vastness and semicircles (fig. 2.2.2); it is followed by a frontal establishing shot of a brown building, which tracks in, pans left, and tilts down to follow the crowd pouring out onto the campus pavement below, revealing crisscrossing lines below the building's horizontal rows of windows (fig. 5.6.2). Even in more defined spaces such as these, cinematic space can mimic the properties of material space, reconfigure it (frontality or verticality within a predominantly circular space), and spill out beyond the material existence of the rectangular film frame.

In spite of its earthly setting and limited number of locales, *Arrival* offers a rich and varied experience of cinematic space, revealing the multitude of configurations enabled by an abstract shape like the Shell or a dark and vacuous void like the chamber. These experiments with cinematic landscape and

Figures 5.6.1–5.6.2. The concrete places of the early scenes are also material that can be reconfigured, rectangular blocks emerging from a track-in in a circular hospital hallway, crisscrossing lines from a track-and-pan-and-tilt shot of the university buildings.

space are enabled by the science fiction material—which provides both a reason for the presence of these shapes and a framework with which to comprehend them—and are never entirely disconnected from its narrative, dramatic, emotional, or symbolic functions. "Landscape," Villeneuve says, "is a very powerful ally, and you can use landscape in a very emotional way."[24] *Arrival* certainly exemplifies the director's awareness of the relations between emotion, places, and landscapes in an audiovisual medium, whether emotions are projected onto (as in the case of pathetic fallacy) or apparently intrinsic to (as in the case of the sublime) a given place or landscape. With its formal experiments grounded in genre and narrative, *Arrival*'s treatment of space is yet another example of how the film steers a course between mainstream blockbuster and art cinema. In the end, the plastic reconfigurations are both a means of telling the story of the heroine's (re)discovery of a nonlinear space-time, and of evoking the crystalline quality of her subjective experience of it. They represent an endeavor to go where no person has gone before, one that is bold and yet doomed to fail, due, in part perhaps, to the limitations imposed by the economic and narrative imperatives attached to the film but, above all, to our own inability to imagine an alien space-time that does not abide by the earthly laws human science has constructed.

Arrival as a Political and Ethical Experience

THE GEOPOLITICAL BACKDROP

In 2016 there was nothing novel about a Hollywood science fiction blockbuster depicting events on a global scale; it has become a staple feature of both the genre and mode of production.[1] But what is more specific to *Arrival*, as well as to *Interstellar* and *Blade Runner 2049*, is how the film delineates a trajectory from the familiar contemporary blockbuster territories of geopolitics and identity politics toward the more unexpected realm of ethical speculation. In the age of globalization, the narratives of twenty-first-century Hollywood blockbusters—*2012* (2009), the Godzilla franchise (2014–), and basically the entire Marvel Cinematic Universe—have depicted natural, supernatural, or cosmic catastrophes threatening the village we call Earth. Since the 1990s, Hollywood has increasingly enlisted foreign talent and/or set its stories around the world in the hopes of conquering foreign markets, East Asian ones in particular (*Pacific Rim* [2013], the Godzilla movies, *The Eternals* [2021], *Shang-Chi and the Legend of the Ten Rings* [2021]).[2]

With its focus on humanity's future and positioning of Earth as a mere speck of dust in the universe, science fiction has long been inclined to pose its questions on a global scale. The alien invasion movie subgenre generally posits that a war of the worlds is or will inevitably become a geopolitical issue, raising the specter of colonization most often directed at those responsible for colonizing other peoples on Earth. Even in its pacifist versions, like *The Day the Earth Stood Still*, the invaders redefine our perception of us versus them, forcing us earthlings to integrate and momentarily set aside our differences; the ensuing human alliance is depicted as fairly easy to achieve when the invasion is brutal, as in the Russian-set *The Darkest Hour* (2011), less so when it isn't, as in *The Day the Earth Stood Still*. Low-budget works relating a lone invasion in a limited setting play on the risk of failing to prevent the menace from spreading, the microcosm representing (a white male version of) the country or the planet, the events a test of humanity's (often reduced to cisgender white men's) ability to survive (the 1956 *Invasion of the Body Snatchers*, *The Thing*). In such cases, the media is regularly used to inform characters and viewers that the problem is, in effect, global (*Earth versus the Flying Saucers*).

The geopolitical backdrop of *Arrival* is thus very much expected and results from a multitiered imperative involving generic conventions and production strategies. Like many contemporary blockbusters, *Arrival* depicts a post–Cold War world where the balance of power has shifted and China now occupies the USSR's former role as second major player alongside the United States; Agent Halpern says General Shang's "call name" is "Big Domino" because "whatever Shang does, at least four nations will follow," and when China eventually declares war on the heptapods, Pakistan, Russia, and Sudan immediately "follow China's lead." David. H. Fleming even muses that, by allowing the Chinese to "becom[e] partly or wholly responsible for saving the white heroes," *Arrival*, like *2012* and *Gravity*, "index[es] perceptions of the (white) West (con)ceding geopolitical control of the future to the Chinese."[3] Endowed with a modest budget by Hollywood blockbuster standards, *Arrival* adopts the 1950s B-movie strategies of limiting the setting and resorting to the media to tell the global story. Louise finds out that "more objects like this have landed in as many as eight other locations around the world" a mere twenty-five seconds after turning on the TV in her lecture hall, and a map featuring the "twelve unidentified objects spread[ing] across the globe" appears on her TV at home (fig. 6.1.1). It is a given that similar situations are presumably unfolding at the other landing sites, and we immediately get the point thanks to our familiarity with images referring both to contemporary reality and science fiction cinema. The crisis demands an international alliance. "We're coordinating with other countries," a US spokeswoman asserts on the radio, and our first introduction to Agent Halpern confirms the tactical necessity by showing him in discussion with his collaborators (fig. 6.1.2).

Heisserer, as we have seen, explains that the "geopolitical panic" has been worked into the narrative to create an escalating "tension," and it is clearly associated with the action movie subplot (analyzed in chapter 2) that reaches the boiling point in act 4. But it also very much contributes to the dramatic tensions and themes developed by the main plot, notably the difficult communication between scientists on the one hand and the military/political spheres on the other. Two instances suggest that collaborations between scientists and the military are becoming increasingly tense worldwide: first when General Shang (in an intercepted phone call Banks translates for

Figures 6.1.1–6.1.2. The map of the twelve Shell locations worldwide appears on Louise's TV screen; later on, Agent Halpern talks with representatives at each location.

Weber) explains that the Chinese "scientist team is attempting to decode the sets" shortly before declaring war on the heptapods, and later when Halpern informs Louise and Ian that "Russia just executed one of their own experts to keep their secrets." The geopolitical backdrop serves as both mirror and frame, reinforcing through contrast the more localized and intimate main plot's dominance in terms of narrative and emotional interest, while asserting through synecdoche its thematic and political relevance in relation to the big picture.

The two occupational groups hold radically opposed views

of international relations. In Bran Nicol's words, "where the humanities is transnational, the military represents the national or international: groups of aligned nationalities all acting in their national interest."[4] This opposition between national(ist) and transnational views, which had already informed films like *The Day the Earth Stood Still*, is voiced in a heated discussion at the dawn of the fourth act, when Louise asserts a humanist view founded on a synecdochal relation—"This is one of twelve. We are part of a larger whole"—which Agent Halpern counters with an aggressively Darwinist perspective: "Or we're one of twelve contestants for the prize." Politically, the international alliance is short-lived (General Shang formulates his ultimatum on Day 27) and was not easy to set up in the first place (a TV host announces on Day 5 that "an agreement on sharing scientific discoveries looks closer tonight as Russia and China join talks at the United Nations"). By comparison, the films' scientists, as Gina Zavota and Pablo Gómez-Muñoz have suggested, hold a cosmopolitan view of a global village working together to try and solve humanity's problems.[5] Cooperation comes easily for them and appears integral to their work. Ian is shown early on exchanging with a British colleague onscreen. And the scientific community's transnationalism is underscored in the popular-documentary sequence even when it fails to provide all the answers: Ian's mention of "the world's most decorated experts" is accompanied by satellite images of Shell locations, the voice of science literally piecing together a fragmented planet; this is shortly followed by the physicist's informing us that "we have our friends in Pakistan to thank for their study of how heptapods write," demonstrating that Pakistani scientists are not on the same wavelength as their nation's leaders shortly before the latter opt to follow China.

The opposition between transnational science and national(ist) politics is made patent in the use of screens. Limited screen time notwithstanding, the international scientists with which the Montana team communicates are individualized; the Australian spokesperson expresses despair ("Really, we—we have nothing"), while Ian's British colleague calls him a "cheeky bastard" in response to his sarcasm. Unlike in films such as *Independence Day*, *Mars Attacks!*, and *Contact*, no direct access is given to politicians, high-ranking military officers, or even average citizens worldwide; all are mediated by cliché-laden words and images of fear: Russia is associated with tanks and missiles on both US and Russian television; Venezuela with social unrest documented with a shaky handheld camera; Pakistan, Sierra Leone, and Sudan with Muslims praying (the fact that it could be any of these countries obviously reinforcing the stereotyping); the United States with guns, looting, and mass suicide; and the United Kingdom with a tagger sporting a Guy Fawkes mask recalling *V for Vendetta* and the Anonymous movement. The constant mediatization justifies and somewhat saves the film's stereotypical representation of geopolitics because the simplified Manichean view we are presented with is, at least partly, an effect of the mass media, one that fails to bring nuance. As Sophie Mayer has noted, the film's "news bulletins are dominated by female presenters of a range of ethnicities when the ships first arrive, but they are replaced by male presenters when a global war footing emerges."[6] In the final act, the images of the imminent war of the worlds are, pointedly, devoid of human beings and depict only war's machines. The clichéd "geopolitical panic" culminates in a sort of Baudrillardian demonstration of the contamination of the real by simulacra, with the media footage unproblematically segueing into images that echo famous movies or video games—the aerial shot of a helicopter rising to attack the Shell straight out of *Apocalypse Now* (1979), the POV shot from within a cockpit recalling a flight simulator (figs. 6.2.1–6.2.3). These final images seem to highlight the fact that the film's depiction of the political/military world is as stereotypical as any other Hollywood blockbuster's, and perhaps more deliberately so. Colonel Weber, as Fleming has argued, is allowed only to embody his "rank within a de-individualising disciplinary organisation";[7] the same can be said of Agent Halpern, and even of Captain Marks, whose backstory serves only to justify his complicity in the action movie subplot.

Louise Banks ultimately manages to jam the war machine by speaking to a human being, the geopolitical subplot's archvillain, General Shang. Heptapod B grants the heroine and the audience (through the flash-forward) access to an actual person (fig. 6.3.2), "a benevolent absent father figure" at that,[8] who had previously been portrayed by US television as a two-dimensional figure in a muted video image (fig. 6.3.1). As Bran Nicol concludes, this addition to the source text allows *Arrival* "to convey a message about the restorative potential of a concerted transnational, indeed transplanetary, feat of translation in the face of a new global threat," introducing a "faith in the more general but still powerful values in human interaction which is at the heart of the practice of translation."[9] Unlike Chiang's heptapods, *Arrival*'s have come not just to "enact or perform what was being said for it to happen,"[10] but to restore faith in humanity's ability to communicate and sow

Figures 6.2.1–6.2.3. A montage sequence cuts directly from media images to clichéd movie and video game images, endowing the images of global war with a hyperreal quality.

the seeds of cosmopolitanism. Yet if Banks's convincing the Chinese general to call off the attack seems to herald the victory of transnational cooperation, the ensuing media images (fig. 4.4) somewhat put a damper on the hopeful outcome. On the one hand, the multiplicity of voices celebrating the fact that "China has said all intelligence they have received will be shared immediately with all the other landing sites," that "scientists from around the world are sifting through information received from the UK, Japan, Sierra Leone, and Venezuela," and that "the twelve pieces of the puzzle" are "being slowly put together" (a reformulation of Louise's words to Halpern) appear as the visual illustration of the cosmopolitan/heptapod perspective; on the other hand, the dominance of English and the film's unflattering portrayal of the infotainment media should serve as a warning that the cosmopolitan potential might just be digested and spat out as another set of clichés.[11] The film thus leaves open-ended the question as to whether or not Louise has succeeded. Geopolitical tensions presumably remain, the future General Shang admitting to Louise Banks that she's the only reason he accepted the US president's invitation. Intimate relationships fare no better, as Ian and Louise's separation suggests. And Fleming even entertains the provocative possibility that Louise Banks herself has been duped by the extraterrestrial colonizers:

> Having Weber embody a black historical montage of colonial encounters *and* give voice to the dominant white/coloniser discourse works to undermine or overturn Banks's so-called breakthrough with the Heptapods. For, as the first human to communicate

Figures 6.3.1–6.3.2. General Shang, characterized by the media as a military dictator, is presented in a warmer light when he introduces himself to Louise at the reception.

> and think in the aliens' new power-knowledge system, Banks essentially internalises alienness in a way comparable to how Weber is shown to have internalised whiteness (or hegemonic notions of white superiority *à la* Fanon).[12]

In deconstructing the binary views it originally seems to uphold and presenting a view of "reverse colonialism" in the form of the generous "blackened" heptapods,[13] *Arrival* seems to preempt potential criticism, which it did in fact receive, regarding the "postfeminist" female lead's role in "normalizing colonial history."[14] But the film's admirable heroine does come with her own lot of limitations.

A WOMAN'S FILM

Amy Adams stated that Denis Villeneuve pitched the project to her by saying, "At the end, it's a mom. A mother. It's just a mother telling a story to her daughter."[15] The idea is better captured by the title of the short story, "Story of Your Life," than by that of the film, which evokes the mother-daughter story through a subtle reference to the hypotext: whereas the verb "arrive" is used by Louise in voice-over and later by Weber to refer to the heptapods, Chiang's narrator uses the corresponding noun to refer to Hannah's birth as early as the end of the first vignette.[16] The change in title serves, first and foremost, a dramatic function. It turns the underlying mother-daughter story into a final reveal, voiced by the epilogue's first words—"So, Hannah. This is where your story begins"—which disclose that the mother's addressee was, from the start, her own daughter and not the generic second-person pronoun of the opening voice-over's final line, which seemed to refer to Louise's own experience: "There are days that define your story beyond your life. Like the day they arrived." *Arrival* was thus intended as a science fiction–woman's film hybrid. If it might have come as a surprise to audiences exclusively familiar with Villeneuve's English-language films featuring troubled and sometimes violent men (*Enemy*, *Prisoners*, *Sicario*), it is very much in line with his French Canadian films, as the director reminded one interviewer,[17] which included female leads and explored themes typical of the woman's film (pregnancy in *Un 32 août sur terre*, abortion in *Maëlstrom*, sexist hate crimes in *Polytechnique*, mother-child relationships in *Incendies*).

A fairly recent generic label, the woman's film is one of Rick Altman's prime examples of genres being more a matter of usage (and thus of pragmatics) than of semantics and syntax.[18] The term was invented in the 1970s by feminist scholars such as Molly Haskell and taken up by the likes of Jeanine Basinger and Mary Ann Doane. In her 1987 *The Desire to Desire*, Doane grouped together films identified in their time as dramas (*Stella Dallas*, 1937), crime films (*Mildred Pierce*, 1945), horror movies (*Cat People*, 1942), and musicals (*Lady in the Dark*, 1944) and foregrounded their narrative, thematic, and ideological commonalities. Basinger sums up the three "purposes" of these films as follows: they place "a woman at the center of the story universe," "provide a temporary visual liberation of some sort, however small—an escape into a purely romantic love, into sexual awareness, into luxury, or into the rejection of the female role," only to "reaffirm in the end the concept that a woman's true job is that of being a woman."[19] The female protagonist is the main focalizer, and the "problems" explored include "domestic life, the family, children, self-sacrifice, and the relationship between woman and production vs. that between women and reproduction."[20] Typically, the protagonist ends up giving up her career (*Female*, 1933), her lover (*Brief Encounter*, 1945), or even her children "for their own good" (*Stella Dallas*). Doane warns that these films do "not provide us with an access to a pure and authentic female subjectivity" but "document a crisis in subjectivity around the figure of the woman—although it is not always clear whose subjectivity is at stake."[21] As male fantasies about women, woman's films tend to be just as heteronormative and male-centric as the male-centered films discussed by Laura Mulvey, albeit more covertly so; like the horror films studied by Carol J. Clover,[22] they are underpinned by male anxieties, more specifically a fear of female subjectivity, and function to "immobilize" and "deny the woman the space of a reading":[23] Doane writes, "We are being subjected to a discourse on femininity."[24] In recent years, the woman's film has been explored and revised by female and male directors alike (Lynne Ramsay's 2013 adaptation of Lionel Shriver's 2003 novel *We Need to Talk about Kevin*,[25] Todd Haynes's 2002 *Far from Heaven* and 2015 *Carol*) in order to tap into the genre's subversive potential while rejecting the return-to-the-status-quo ending (Basinger's second and third purposes). *Arrival* certainly touches on several themes that have been identified as common to the woman's film: being a woman in a "man's world," the potentially incompatible roles of mother and professional, the sacrifices women make. Unlike *Sicario*, in which the heroine, played by Emily Blunt, is ultimately ejected from the hypermasculine action plot, *Arrival* maintains Louise as the main focalizer (i.e., the narrative's cognitive center) throughout the film with very few exceptions,[26] leaving center stage to Ian Donnelly only in the popular-science sequence that celebrates her work.[27] It remains to be seen to what extent the 2016 film proposes a critical revision of the woman's film.

This generic blend is one of the film's main novelties. As Helen Merrick remarks in her chapter "Gender and Science Fiction" in *The Cambridge Companion to Science Fiction*, "sf has long been considered a predominantly masculine field which, through its focus on science and technology, 'naturally' excludes women and, by implication, considerations of gender."[28] And while there is abundant female-authored and -centered science fiction literature, and even cases like Suzy McKee Charnas's *Motherlines* (1978) and Sally Miller Gearhart's *The Wanderground* (1980) in which "'women' equals human" in a world without men,[29] science fiction cinema has traditionally been a male-centered genre.[30] Classical Hollywood science fiction movies largely position female characters as love interests or sidekicks (*The Day the Earth Stood Still*, *The Man from Planet X*, *Earth versus the Flying Saucers*),[31] even when they are depicted as brainy (Joyce Handron, the professor's daughter in *When Worlds Collide*, is shown at work making measurements only to be relegated to the role of love interest shortly thereafter). As a contemporary science fiction film centered on a female scientist, *Arrival* follows the lead of *Gravity*,[32] *The Thing* (van Heijningen, 2011), *eXistenZ* (Cronenberg, 1999), and especially *Contact* (1997). A comparison between the posters of the 1997 and 2016 films is particularly enlightening. *Contact*'s displays Jodie Foster's name above Matthew McConaughey's, but the male actor and the satellite dish loom over the female star, suggesting that McConaughey's role will be far more important than it actually turns out to be. In spite of Foster's impressive credentials—a twenty-five-year-long movie career and an Academy Award for *The Silence of the Lambs* (1991)—the marketing team did not bank on her to carry a science fiction film without a male counterpart, even if the latter is played by a lesser-known actor who had just pulled off his first leading role a year before in *A Time to Kill* (1996). By comparison, Amy Adams, with the Shell and her male costars gravitating around her, unquestionably dominates the US poster of *Arrival*, in what is ultimately her first leading role after a string of supporting ones. In 2013, the team behind *Gravity* was apparently not willing to take the same risk: A-list star Sandra Bullock notwithstanding, the US poster emphasizes action by depicting an anonymous astronaut falling into space.

Heisserer jokes that Jeremy Renner is essentially the "Ginger Rogers of the movie,"[33] and in the chamber scenes, Ian follows Louise Banks's instructions more obediently even than Lisa Fremont and nurse Stella follow L. B. Jefferies's in *Rear Window*. Sophie Mayer nonetheless deplores the idea that "*Arrival* does not appear to realize" that such "gender trouble is not enough";[34] she takes particular issue with the presence of a lone female lead who goes from teaching the heptapods the word "human" to first names without touching on gender.[35] Upon her arrival in Montana, Louise enters a military world where the key positions are occupied by men (Colonel Weber, the CIA agent, the army doctor, the personnel who assist Louise and Ian), and on Louise and Ian's first visit to the camp, we glimpse few women (two in the medical ward; one in the monitoring room; three representing Denmark, China, and the United States on Halpern's screens; one military scientist on Ian's team; three on Louise's team), who are generally engulfed in shadow and/or relegated to the background or sides of the frame. This is particularly salient as recent representations of the US military in war and science fiction movies tend to emphasize the presence of women officers and soldiers (*Home of the Brave*, 2006; *Megan Leavey*, 2017; *The Predator*, 2018). The gender disparity seems to be justified by the persistence of systemic sexism within the military, which is hinted at when Louise and the audience discover that a "guy" named Dr. Walker was their first choice. It is also audible on the recording Weber plays in her office: the soundtrack of the classic alien invasion scene is initially dominated by a disembodied male voice, in a neat illustration of Kaja Silverman's thesis that "at its most crudely dichotomous, Hollywood pits the disembodied male voice against the synchronized female voice" (in this case, Louise's).[36]

Arrival quite deliberately enforces the stereotypical association of men with physical strength and women with intellect or care. This is furthered by the equally gendered opposition between physics and the humanities that is introduced from the outset, with Ian leading the way at the Montana base and being introduced to his team first. The tensions between hard science fiction and action sci-fi on the one hand, and linguistics and physics on the other, are thus gendered and present Louise as a (quasi-)lone woman in a man's world, very much like *Sicario*'s Kate Macer, who is enlisted in an all-male task force. The only woman present at the decisive moments (the Shell visits and the meetings), Louise Banks is characterized, as Mayer implies, as an exceptional woman. The strategies used to take linguistics seriously (analyzed in chapter 2) also work to take women—or at least this one—seriously; her gender is never brought up in conversation, and none of the male characters indulge in mansplaining or other condescending attitudes (yet again unlike *Sicario*). By documenting the laborious stages and insisting on the methodological and theoretical logic of the collective effort that goes into the translation process (examined in chapter 3), *Arrival* demonstrates that Louise's successes cannot be put down to female intuition (and this in spite of the director's own valuation of "intuition" over language[37]). And unlike Eleanor Arroway in *Contact*, Louise is not portrayed as a hysterical woman no one will listen to unless a man is there to second her (by comparison, the Chinese spokeswoman on the diegetic screen is accompanied by a spokesman). *Arrival* thus carefully avoids these two tropes that patriarchal ideologies have historically associated with femininity.[38]

Louise Banks is, however, presented as exceptional per se as early as her first meeting with Colonel Weber, the scene that sets up the first-contact mission premise. She is "on the top of everyone's lists when it comes to translations" and is more competent, as it turns out, than her counterpart at UC Berkeley, a man named Danvers. The scene also endows her with a secondary motive of the Jason Bourne kind: it informs us that the insurgents whose videos she translated were subsequently eliminated, establishing this second US military mission as a sort of sequel with redemptive potential, with Louise putting her life at risk to avoid bloodshed. The linguist's exceptional abilities are confirmed as soon as the second Shell visit, when she sets herself apart from all the male characters, relegated to the middle and background, thereby confirming the promise of the movie poster. If her prowess is above all cerebral, she is better adapted to tolerating the chamber's atmosphere than Ian, who retches in the decontamination room, and especially Dr. Walker, who may have been the person being "carted off in the medevac" upon Louise and Ian's arrival at the camp. Louise Banks is an "action-image hero" working to save the world,[39] a classical hero with a clear-cut motive and deadline, whose actions and decisions energize the plot at every stage.[40]

She corresponds only partly to the 1990s "action women" or "female heroes" discussed by Yvonne Tasker and Christine Cornea, who were "constructed in narrative terms as macho/masculine, as mothers or as Others."[41] Her body is not fetishized in the manner of Sarah Connor, Jill in *Hardware* (1990),[42] or twenty-first-century cinematic superheroines, and her intellectual abilities are coded as "masculine" only insofar as the scientific community is presented as mainly composed of men. She is, however, immediately presented as a mother and a linguist, in that order, with the fade-to-black separating the prologue from the main body of the film, one function from the other—Louise now inhabits the dark corridors of a university after saying goodbye to her daughter Hannah in the silver-blue corridors of the hospital. On a first viewing, Louise Banks is available because she is childless, so, unlike Cooper in *Interstellar*, she doesn't have to worry about whether her mission will compromise her role as a parent. The woman's film tension between career and personal life is thus avoided. It returns with a vengeance, fulfilling the heart-rending prologue's promise, when the flashes of Hannah start occurring: Louise now seems to embody the exemplary woman's film heroine, increasingly perturbed by her troubled mind, which now threatens to compromise her work. The classical woman's film reading is canceled out only when Louise shares her incomprehension with Costello in their final meeting: "I don't . . . understand. Who is this child?" (figs. 6.4.1–6.4.2). While the revelation that the prologue was actually a flash-forward reframes what could previously have been interpreted as vulnerability (the heroine coming mentally unhinged) as a strength ("Louise has weapon"), it does not annul Louise's status as mother. Borrowing from Barbara Duden's description of the fetus's status as "not-yet" in the sense of neither dead nor alive,[43] Anne Carruthers astutely argues that Louise's experience exemplifies the idea that pregnancy also affects maternal subjectivity, creating a temporality that is "'not-yet' maternal."[44] The narrative's time paradox makes it so that Louise is always a mother even when she isn't, and thus that the mother-daughter relationship remains the heart of the movie throughout.

Is this enough to argue that *Arrival* is an instance of female subjectivity and not male subjectivity in disguise? Carruthers makes the bold claim that the film invites us to experience a sort of "pregnant embodiment," a notion she borrows from Iris Marion Young.[45] Carruthers notes that some of the symptoms experienced by Louise and Ian recall those provoked by pregnancy—Ian vomits after the first visit, and Louise is "doubled up" when overwhelmed by the first visions and tries to pace her breathing.[46] This more corporeal manifestation of gender trouble is also patent in the blood test scene, when the hands working the syringe turn out to be the female nurse's and not Dr. Kettler's (fig. 3.5.2). Carruthers's argument also reminds us that, on a second viewing at least, the film's gendered terms should be perceived as filtered by the protagonist's subjectivity. In this light, the stereotypical representation of the camp's sociological makeup may inform us more of Louise's mental state than of the actual state of the US military in 2016. What ultimately matters is that Louise experienced her time at the military camp as one of being submerged in an all-male world, a world in which she, quite possibly, felt, like many real-life women, that she had to assert her competence all the more because of her gender.[47]

In the end, it can always be argued that *Arrival*'s representation of women and expression of female subjectivity are by no means "pure" because they were produced by a predominantly male team and tap into familiar tropes, but an effort has been made to deconstruct the latter. Louise is presented as a loving but probably imperfect parent (she doesn't have all the answers and gets her share of "I hate you"s); more importantly, her identity cannot be reduced to that function. More original, perhaps, is that *Arrival* does not explore motherhood as a social status so much as a physical and emotional experience. Choosing between one's personal life and career is not of dramatic interest, and the non-zero-sum game scenes show Louise taking time to help Hannah while working. The woman's film trope of self-sacrifice is thus displaced onto another, more metaphysical plane: knowing the bleak outcome, Louise paradoxically chooses self-sacrifice so as not to sacrifice life. In this twenty-first-century science fiction woman's film, the female scientist's fate is not melodramatic but tragic, and it has very little to do with ideology and everything to do with ethics.

MORAL DILEMMAS, ETHICAL ENCOUNTERS

"Despite knowing the journey and where it leads, I embrace it. And I welcome every moment of it." The voice-over's final words celebrate a carpe diem or "quasi-Buddhist" view of life[48] that justifies the heroine's decision to love Ian and have Hannah despite her knowledge that her daughter will die of cancer and her husband will leave her because she withheld that crucial piece of information. Pursuing the legacy of Aristotle's *Nicomachean Ethics*, Charles Taylor and Paul Ricœur insist on the idea that life is an ethical experience, the French philosopher defining "ethical intention" as "aiming at the 'good life' with and for others, in just institutions,"[49] and the Canadian philosopher describing the good life as "one which somehow combines to the greatest possible degree all the goods we seek."[50] Louise's decision is profoundly ethical because it is an assertion that Hannah's and her lives will be worth living, that the goods will outweigh the pain and suffering: "Your swimming and your poetry and all the amazing things that you share with the world." Her foresight of the darkness to come endows the film (like *Interstellar*) with a "tragic resonance" or "dimension," as Bréan and Gervais have noted,[51] which the film's musical frame, Max Richter's "On the Nature of Daylight," largely contributes to underscore. Yet Louise differs from the classical tragic figure because of her awareness of the consequences of her decision, so it is ultimately Ian whose fate is tinged with dramatic irony.

Most analyses of the ethics of *Arrival* focus on the ending's moral dilemma, and understandably so. And yet, another such dilemma is stated from the outset: Louise's decision to tell her daughter her story. On a first viewing, in which Louise's voice-over appears to be referring to her own story, the life-changing event seems contingent and entirely exterior to her, but by the end of the film, whose final words are Louise's positive response to Ian's invitation to "make a baby," it becomes clear that the core of the story revolves around how Louise came to decide to have Hannah anyway: the story of Louise's choice is, more profoundly, the sharing of her view of the good life. If the voice-over may be localized at any moment given Louise's relation to time, pragmatically speaking it can make sense only from the perspective of the addressee if the information is shared with Hannah after her diagnosis and before her death—otherwise, Louise would merely be telling the story to herself. The prologue seems to lend weight to the first hypothesis: the order of the events suggests that Hannah's "I hate you" is her reaction to her mother's story, an interpretation reinforced by her look to the camera, as if the narratee were struggling to reach us through the mother's narrative and

Figures 6.4.1–6.4.2. In the prologue, a teenage Hannah screams, "I hate you!" at the camera (and presumably at her mother), a cry that, on second viewing, we could interpret as her reaction to her mother's foreknowledge of her fatal cancer. During Louise's final conversation with Costello beyond the window, Hannah's identity is revealed to be a mystery to her mother, who asks, "Who is this child?"

the film's narration and tell her side of the story (fig. 6.4.1). Of course, the prologue's fragmented narration does not impose a one-track causality, and consequently leaves room for doubt: Hannah's words could be just a random outbreak of anger, and Louise really could be just telling the story to herself. The latter possibility would imply that Louise actually is a tragic figure whose hubris led her to make a selfish decision, and that the choice she embraces is that of a self who decides in place of others, as the repetition of the first person pronoun suggests. In this light, Louise's decision could appear problematic, since she also chose a life for—and not "with," as in Ricœur's definition—others. *Arrival* leaves open-ended the question as to whether Louise's decisions to have and to tell were good ones. While Ian's absence in the flashes is enough to inform us that he did not adhere to his wife's view of the good life ("I told him something that he wasn't ready to hear," Louise tells her daughter), we do not know whether Hannah came to terms with it; all we know is that mother and daughter remained together to the bitter end.

But the film's ethical implications delve far beyond the moral questions about whether a life is worth living and a story is worth telling. Tapping into Jacques Lacan's ethics of psychoanalysis, Scott Krzych briefly describes Louise Banks as an instance of the "ethical sublime," the flashes depicting her as aware of her loss and yet joyful.[52] Evoking Donna J. Haraway's notion of the "chthulucene," David H. Fleming and William Brown echo this view, stating that "change with(in) time . . . would be ethically to accept the universe and the cosmic."[53] For Francesco Sticchi, "the film demonstrates how communication relies on interactive, dynamic, and empathic ethical activities,"[54] and its protagonist, in her relationship with the heptapods and others in general, enacts "a Spinozistic pragmatic ethics, one that looks for new ways of generating and affirming a positive interaction among beings, and consequently defines the possibility of transforming ourselves and our capacity to relate to other individuals."[55] And for Gina Zavota, *Arrival* illustrates three of Jacques Derrida's theories, including the idea that a "genuine" gift should remain "aneconomic" and not elicit a "countergift" or "debt"; though given in exchange for services rendered by humanity three thousand years from now, the heptapods' gift of language ultimately escapes the debt-creating economy of gift-making because the nonlinear narrative places Louise "outside the circular economy of giving and reciprocation."[56] In a sense, the heptapods' true gift would be the new relation to time Heptapod B opens onto because it makes "true altruism and meaningful political exchange possible."[57] These illuminating interpretations prove not only that the film's "open-ended incoherence . . . invites compulsive and arcane readings,"[58] sometimes based on conflicting philosophical frameworks, but also that its ethical concerns involve the alien invasion plot and its theme of communication just as much as the family melodrama frame story.

Arrival entertains the idea that an alien language could feed back into, and profoundly alter, one's consciousness. Ian first wonders whether Heptapod B's "nonlinear orthography" is an indication of "how they think" during the documentary sequence. The possibility is again touched on in the dream sequence, when Ian mentions the Sapir-Whorf hypothesis, according to which "if you immerse yourself into a foreign language, then you can actually rewire your brain," and Louise sums up the theory thus: "The language you speak—determines how you think and . . . affects how you see everything." While the physicist's description evokes a fairly basic version of cognitive psychology's perception-cognition-action schema,[59] with a cognitive modification leading to changes in perception and motor action, the linguist's response calls on other frameworks through the usage of two verbs: contemporary "affect" theory and the long philosophical tradition of metaphysics, whose definition of the verb "see" is not limited to visual perception. Significantly, the second verb is also used by Costello in the first stage of the climax, when he explains to Louise the nature of the gift bestowed upon her: "Louise sees future." Her newfound view of the "good life" stems from this change, since, like Costello, for whom "Abbott is death process," Louise will come to see past, present, and future, life and death, as precariously occupying the same plane of immanence (see chapter 4)—the use of the present tense insists on her ability in general rather than her acquiring and wielding it in the now. But it is not so much Louise's brain that has evolved as her ethical view. The second climax drives in the point when Louise describes her final mission to convince General Shang to call off the attack on the Shell as "changing someone's mind," citing the Chinese officer's own words. If Louise now finds herself in the heptapods' position, the second stage of the film's climax thus replaying the first, the aim of her phone call is obviously not to rewire the general's brain but to ask him to make a political decision based on what Charles Taylor calls a "hypergood"—in other words, "a good which challenges and displaces others" and "which makes us see others differently"[60]—formulated in Shang's "wife's dying words." If Heisserer's interviews happily translated these words as "In wars, there are no winners, only widows,"[61] the lack of subtitles suggests that it is not the words themselves that matter so much as the communication context; it also contrasts with their presence to translate and undoubtedly simplify Heptapod B during Louise and Costello's final conversation.[62] The asymmetry between both scenes may actually highlight a parallel: the inadequacy of words to fully convey the profundity of these exchanges. The final meeting between Louise and Shang thus draws attention to the ethical foundations not only of her final encounter with Costello but of all her interactions with the heptapods.

In many respects, the film's original approach to the first-contact premise resonates with the main tenets of Emmanuel Levinas's moral philosophy. The famous starting point of the French philosopher's seminal 1961 *Totality and Infinity* is his reaction to World War II: the realization that "the state of war suspends morality" and "renders [it] derisory," and that it makes manifest the dominance of "the concept of totality" and the practice of ontological theorizing in Western philosophy's interrogation of "being."[63] Instead, Levinas makes a case for ethics as the foundation of philosophical inquiry and metaphysics as its central practice: ethics, "the relationship of man to man," "accomplishes the critical essence of knowledge."[64] With "totality," Levinas contrasts the concept of "Infinity," which "is produced in the relationship of the same with the other" and is the "condition for every opinion as also for every objective truth."[65] Levinas describes this encounter as a "face to face" that "founds" both "language" and "signification."[66] The Other must be recognized as "absolutely other"[67] and not posited as eventually contained within the same (as in immanent views)—thus, the "separation" inherent in the idea of infinity can never be entirely bridged.[68] Levinas calls this otherness of the Other "face [*visage*]," a face that goes beyond the physical face: "The face of the Other destroys at each moment and overflows the plastic image it leaves me, the idea existing to my own measure and to the measure of its *ideatum*—the adequate idea."[69] The relationship between Same and Other is not immanent but transcendent,[70] not in the sense that one could transcend one's condition through the Other but in recognition that the Other is also a master who "judges me" and "commands me" in this relationship.[71] This recognition leads me to give up my "egoist spontaneity," for "to recognize the Other is to give,"[72] an idea that foreshadows Derrida's reflections on the economics of gift-giving.

The first-contact narrative is potentially one in which humans come face-to-face with absolute otherness against a background of cosmic war. In *Arrival*, the separation between human and heptapod is materialized by the window, of course, but more radically by the different atmospheres they inhabit, which limit both the frequency and the duration of their encounters, since the earthly atmosphere inside the Shell antechamber and chamber needs to be replenished every eighteen hours. But the separation remains even when Louise penetrates the Shell. Indeed, the heptapods' otherness is figured by their Lovecraftian/Cephalopoda bodies, their "blackness," which stands out all the more in their silver-white environment, and their lack of "anthropomorphic" features.[73] Even in the final encounter, the reverse shots of the central and top of Costello's body express both Louise's and the narration's effort and failure to locate a physical face (figs. 6.5.1–6.5.2). The heptapods thus come to figure an absolute Other whose face cannot be reduced to a form. And yet the shot/reverse shots not only express the attempt to communicate and establish a relationship with the Other, as explored in chapter 3; the classical dialogue device consecrates the "face" of the Other in spite of the absence of a physical face. For Louise, Ian, and the audience, Abbott and Costello are eventually individuated in spite of the lack of a face (Louise has no trouble recognizing them). The "face-to-face" is thus visually expressed through staging and editing.

The soundtrack plays a key role in suggesting that the face-to-face is not a mere matter of just facing each other. The heptapods' otherness is audible in the radical otherness

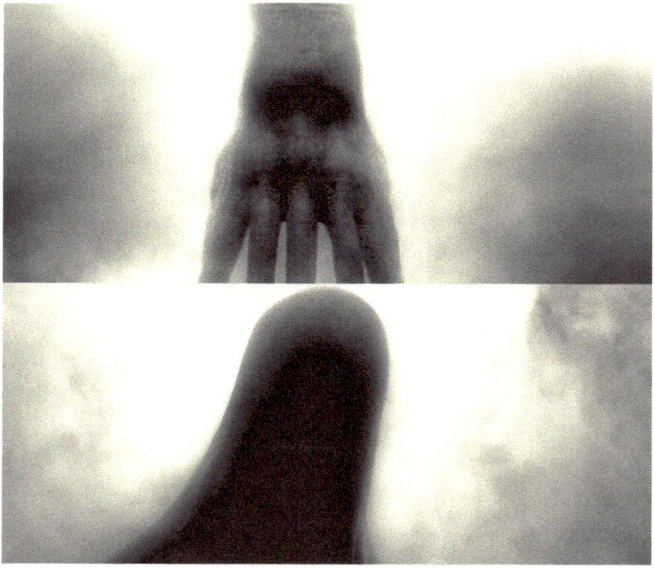

Figures 6.5.1–6.5.2. Beyond the window: Costello's body resists Louise's attempt to identify his physical face, a resistance that further constitutes the heptapod as "the face of the Other."

of Heptapod A; it is not always clear whether the sounds they produce are words or noises, and their voices and language (which Louise admits to being physically incapable of ever speaking) register as noise or music on the humans' equipment (Weber's recorder, the decibel gauges). This radical otherness is furthered, during the alien encounter scenes, by the blurring of the voice-noise-music triad (again, the heptapods' voices, but also Jóhannsson's score, which sometimes sounds like the heptapods). In effect, the visual motif of the window as border is compromised by the various sounds spilling outside of—and thus transgressing—both the spatial frame (the aliens can be heard through the window) and the fictional frame (because of the blurring between diegetic and nondiegetic sounds).

The encounter is not only physical but metaphysical. It is an opportunity to learn from the Other, to recognize the heptapods as masters, to derive truth from the exchange. The ethical dimension of this encounter is by no means limited to the transmission of a certain view of the good life; it is the foundation of all Louise's interactions with the heptapods. While such an interpretation would seem to exploit the allegorical potential of the alien to figure as absolute Other, the analogy is effectively built into the narrative. Indeed, the metaphysical basis of the heptapod encounters sheds light on the ethical dimension of Louise's other interactions. Louise's two-tiered meeting with General Shang is also a face-to-face with a stranger, in which the officer's face appears to be more than the form relayed by the mass media (fig. 6.3.1); this time, Louise privileges two-way communication via a phone rather than spying on a phone conversation using the military's satellite technology. The first and second stages of the climax yet again mirror each other, both demonstrating that true knowledge can be achieved only through an encounter with the Other founded on generosity. Less obvious encounters with the Other are Louise's visions, the scientist revealing to Costello (of all "people") that she has been flooded with images of an unknown child. Though seeing Hannah in her mind's eye, Louise first meets her daughter as "this child" (the use of the deictic indicating both closeness and distance through verbal pointing), thereby debunking the mythical view of the child as an emanation of the parent. Hannah's looks to the camera operate similarly as the reverse shots of the heptapods (fig. 6.5): they are images of the face of the Other, one that has presence in spite of Louise's precarious memories and the film's poetics of blur. Significantly, the ensuing images of Hannah (fig. 4.2.3) are accompanied by low sounds resembling the heptapods' voices that are yet again part of Jóhannsson's score, the child's otherness being thus expressed, like the heptapods', through the blurring of the voice-music-noise triad. Even the romance that concludes the film can be analyzed in a similar light when Ian compares his meetings with Louise and the heptapods: "You know I've had my head tilted up to the stars for as long as I can remember. You know what surprised me the most? It wasn't meeting them. It was meeting you" (fig. 6.6.2). Unlike the vast majority of cinematic alien invasions, the heptapods' arrival enables us to see not the species sameness of human beings but their rich otherness, even that of one's lover or child.

Heptapod B turns out to be a Derridean "gift" of pure altruism, one that could spark metaphysical revelations within a multitude of relations between Same and Other, a cautious hopefulness captured by the two-bar arpeggio melody of "On the Nature of Daylight," which ascends for one measure before repeating a fifth for the next. The film does not, however, naively suggest that such moments are easy to achieve and preserve, as Richter's minor key and modest orchestration remind us. In his 1968 "Substitution," Levinas declares that communication is characterized by "incertitude": "Communication with the other can be transcendence only as a dangerous life, as a fine risk to be run."[74] Thus, communication implies not the actualization of a relationship but its possibility. As Louise confesses in her first intimate conversation with Ian, "you can understand communication and still end up single." Ironically, it is her future, not her past, that ultimately demonstrates her

Figures 6.6.1–6.6.2. Ian appears as a spectral presence in the flashes of Louise's life with Hannah. At the end of the film, the stargazer romantically declares that meeting her surprised him more than meeting the heptapods.

point. In choosing not to adhere to her view of the "good life," Ian asserts his otherness. His face haunts the images of Louise's life with Hannah as an offscreen presence—a blurry figure outside her windows, which Louise, like Abbott, knocks on to get her interlocutor's attention (fig. 6.6.1)—a voice or a face emerging from the blurry background of a lateral close-up of Louise. Louise's command of languages might allow her to convince the military that her way is the right way, but it will fail to win her partner over to her view of the good life, as he remains, like Cooper in *Interstellar*, interested in "star stuff" to the very end. Moreover, by titling her book on Heptapod B *The Universal Language*, Louise seems to fall into the science fiction trap of considering that such a thing as a universal language could exist in the first place—although her sarcastic comment regarding the rhetoric of her previous book's preface, which Ian reads out loud in the helicopter, suggests that the new title could be a matter of marketing and that the book's contents might qualify the simplistic view formulated by the title. Further irony at Louise's expense is hinted at by the possibility that "her accession to cosmic understanding" may very well, as Longfellow puts it, have "been translated into a Realpolitik of banal liberal internationalism."[75] All this does not bode well for the "unification" Louise and the heptapods brought about eighteen months later—and the mention of the number of months by General Shang, who reluctantly accepted the US president's invitation, invites us to conjecture that the newfound world order is as precarious as access to the Shell.

Philosophically speaking, it is interesting to note the apparent contradiction posed by the film's treatment of communication and time: a transcendent encounter with the Other (Levinas) collides with the immanent view of time as subjectivity (Bergson, Deleuze) discussed in chapter 4. And yet I would argue that, like the Derridean gift in Zavota's reading, the immanent view actually serves to maintain the radical separation that defines the relation with the Other. Indeed, it is because of the precariousness of Louise's mental images that the faces we glimpse—Hannah's, Shang's, Ian's—remain absolutely and evidently other, mediated as they are by her subjectivity. The use of flashes makes us very much aware that what we are given to see are the forms these faces take in Louise's consciousness; they are the Other within the Same, echoing Levinas's observation that "childship is even more mysterious: it is a relation with an Other in which the Other is radically Other, and yet is, in a way, me."[76] The radical otherness is evoked in the fact that Louise neither recognizes Hannah ("Who is this child?") nor remembers that she already spoke to Shang on the phone ("And what's that?"). The daughter's and the general's otherness are thus preserved because they remain radically separated from Louise's subjectivity, evoked only as a potential through questions that beg answers from an absent interlocutor. The film thus suggests, as Jaunas concludes, that "complete identification with the other" can exist only as a fantasy.[77] Ethically speaking, the lack of omniscience and the crystalline regime (analyzed in chapter 4) preclude totality and safeguard infinity: the Other is never entirely known and never incorporated into the Same.

Arrival is intensely aware of the hackneyed material it is working with (chapter 2), whether this concerns the geopolitical backdrop indispensable for any contemporary science fiction movie, the sensitive racial and colonial implications attached to the first-contact narrative, or the patriarchal ideology underlying the classical woman's film and classical cinema in general. The film avoids some conventions (the character archetypes of the woman's film), parodies others while working them into the main narrative and themes (the mostly mediatized images of Heisserer's "geopolitical panic"), and even attempts to express the experience of "pregnant embodiment." Geopolitics (Shang's final decision) and gender politics (the frame story centered on Louise and Hannah's life) are put in the service of the "laboratory of moral judgement" that any narrative can be, according to Ricœur.[78] The heptapods' baffling absence of violence displaces the habitual geopolitics of colonization underpinning the alien invasion subgenre in favor of the ethics of the encounter with radical otherness, including humanity's own. An initiation story of the *Close Encounters* kind, *Arrival* relates how such an encounter can modify one's worldview and possibly the world itself. The film's potential limitations thus become attributable not only to the heroine's own—Louise is not the melodramatic heroine of the classical woman's film whose sacrifice reinforces patriarchy, but a tragic heroine whose sacrifice comes with its lot of uncertainties—but, above all, to the limitations of both subjectivity and humanity. In this respect, the film is eminently Levinasian inasmuch as it asserts the primacy of ethics over politics, a hierarchy implicit in the French philosopher's statement that "idealism completely carried out reduces all ethics to politics."[79] For the arrival does have political implications, and not just as an instance of "reverse colonialism." As Brenda Longfellow astutely concludes,

> This reversal does a number of things: it undermines species aggrandisement which considers the human as the pinnacle of evolution, and relativises humanity as but one form of life that exists in a much larger cosmic frame of multiplicity and difference. . . . The reversal privileges another mode of being and ordering relations with others, based in generosity, reciprocity and the primacy of the gift.[80]

Ethics, the film seems to assert, are not disconnected from politics; they are its very foundation. To live with others is to recognize the precious gift of their otherness and the necessity to welcome them in our ideas of the good life.

Conclusion

By proclaiming the validity of the mainstream art film and claiming the status, *Arrival* aims to bring various pleasures and audiences together and assert their equal legitimacy. Its treatment of the science fiction genre and of the themes of communication and space provide ample proof that narrative and spectacle, as Geoff King would have it, need not be opposed but are aesthetic priorities that not only coexist but play off each other (making linguistics interesting entails making the discipline spectacular). Its elaborate handling of narrative structure and narration, time and space, is ample proof that formal experimentation is not the exclusive domain of art and experimental cinema, and that multiple points of convergence (haptic aesthetics, embodied spectatorship) exist between contemporary art and mainstream cinema. A film whose central theme is communication, *Arrival* is about establishing relations between polar opposites, in terms of industrial categories (mainstream and art cinema), of genre (action sci-fi and hard science fiction, science fiction and woman's film), of spectatorial positions (conscious and unconscious, cognition and sensation), and of philosophical perspectives (self and other, transcendent and immanent conceptions of ontology). Eminently meta, it is about the successful encounter between mainstream and art, and it affirms that a mainstream film can have as much to say about cinema as an art film.

This is not the incoherent heterogeneity whose economic aim is to complacently accommodate contradictions in the name of economic imperatives, but a coherent—if complex and ambiguous—heterogeneity in which different sensibilities and aesthetic regimes, like the cosmopolitan academic world depicted in the film, work together: the action movie tropes to structure and energize a hard science narrative; the immanent handling of time to ensure the transcendence of the relation between the self and the Other. In this respect, *Arrival* is the spitting image of its heroine, Dr. Louise Banks, whose subjectivity not only lends the film its crystalline regime but mirrors the film's claim to englobe heterogeneity and paradox, and whose hybrid worldview and fragmented omniscience mirror the experience of both artists and audiences who recognize that endings are actually beginnings, that a given work overflows any claim to authorship, and that even an apparently closed-circuit mind-game film remains an "open" work in which "a great variety of potential meanings coexist" that can never be fully comprehended.[1] Therein lies the ethics of *Arrival*: in the recognition that the work, like the Other, remains transcendent, even for its makers.

Acknowledgments

My first thanks obviously go to my friend Donna Kornhaber, who warmly encouraged me to submit a book proposal to her 21st Century Film Essentials collection and convinced me that *Arrival* was the perfect fit for me and the collection. I'd also like to thank Jim Burr for his enthusiasm and patience, Mia Uribe Kozlovsky for her work on the images, Sarah Hudgens for her careful copyediting, and the rest of the team at the University of Texas Press for their support on this project from beginning to end. I'm grateful for the readers' reports, whose comments helped me (I hope!) improve the manuscript.

I owe the Institut Universitaire de France a lot for endowing me with a grant that largely facilitated the writing of this manuscript.

My eternal gratitude to the friends who read the manuscript and made useful suggestions: Donna, of course, and Claire Cornillon, Antoine Gaudin, and Sarah Hatchuel. I hope the book does justice to this film that we love so very much. I'd also like to thank my PhD candidate, Guilhem Billaudel, who is working on contemporary space movies including *Arrival*—Guilhem, I do hope I haven't stolen any of your ideas! Warm thanks are due to our librarians at University Paul Valéry Montpellier 3, Sandra Blachon in particular. Thanks also to Chloé Delaporte for a useful reference on Hollywood economics, to Virginie Iché for what she considers to be very basic references to linguistic manuals, to Fabien Meynier for introducing me to the work of Yi-Fu Tuan, and to Amandine D'Azevedo for lending me Liu Cixin's *Three-Body Problem* trilogy, my constant companion throughout this book-writing adventure.

Thanks, as always, to my friends, my brother and sister, and my wife and children.

Notes

INTRODUCTION

1. King, *Quality Hollywood*, 6–7.
2. King, *Quality Hollywood*, 12.
3. King, *Quality Hollywood*, 67, 4, 26.
4. King, *Quality Hollywood*, 2, 28.
5. King, *Quality Hollywood*, 29, 46–52.

ARRIVAL AS AUTEUR FILM ADAPTATION

1. "Amy Adams on Denis Villeneuve's 'Arrival'"; "OSCAR-Nominated ARRIVAL screenwriter Eric Heisserer extended interview."
2. "DP/30: Arrival, Eric Heisserer."
3. "DP/30: Arrival, Eric Heisserer."
4. "DP/30: Arrival, Eric Heisserer."
5. "Amy Adams on Denis Villeneuve's 'Arrival.'"
6. "Denis Villeneuve on How He Directed Arrival."
7. "Science Fiction News: Actor David Dastmalchian Joins Villeneuve's Dune Reboot," The Movie Sleuth, February 19, 2019, https://www.spoilerfreemoviesleuth.com/2019/02/science-fiction-news-actor-david.html?m=0; Dan Cooper, "Trailer Lands for Denis Villeneuve's Dune," Film Stories, September 10, 2020, https://filmstories.co.uk/news/trailer-lands-for-denis-villeneuves-dune; Kyle Pinion, "Why I Wish I Hadn't Read Dune before I Watched It," Screenrex, October 19, 2021, https://screenrex.com/dune.
8. Jacques Morice, "Denis Villeneuve: 'Prisoners' est un film douloureusement américain, proche d'un Western,"

Telerama, October 8, 2013, https://www.telerama.fr/cinema/denis-villeneuve-prisoners-est-un-film-douloureusement-americain-proche-d-un-western,103305.php; Adam Chitwood, "Production Begins on Denis Villeneuve's Thriller PRISONERS, Starring Hugh Jackman and Jake Gyllenhaal," Collider, February 20, 2013, https://collider.com/production-begins-on-denis-villeneuves-thriller-prisoners-starring-hugh-jackman-and-jake-gyllenhaal.

9. "Amy Adams on Denis Villeneuve's 'Arrival.'"
10. "DP/30: Arrival, Eric Heisserer."
11. "OSCAR-Nominated ARRIVAL screenwriter Eric Heisserer extended interview."
12. "DP/30: Arrival, Denis Villeneuve."
13. "DP/30: Arrival, Eric Heisserer."
14. "DP/30: Arrival, Eric Heisserer."
15. "DP/30: Arrival, Eric Heisserer."
16. "Arrival (film)," Wikipedia, https://en.wikipedia.org/wiki/Arrival_(film)#Development_and_pre-production, accessed September 22, 2022.
17. "DP/30: Arrival, Denis Villeneuve."
18. Elsaesser, "A Retrospect."
19. *Arrival*, Blu-ray (Sony Pictures, 2017).
20. "DP/30: Arrival, Denis Villeneuve."
21. "DP/30: Arrival, Denis Villeneuve."
22. "Filming in Quebec," The Location Guide, https://www.thelocationguide.com/locations/quebec; Ian Austen, "The Canadians Behind 'Dune,'" *New York Times*, October 29, 2021, https://www.nytimes.com/2021/10/29/world/canada/dune-movie.html.
23. Sellors, "Collective Authorship in Film," 269.
24. Sellors, "Collective Authorship in Film," 269.
25. The Blu-ray DVD extras are titled "Eternal Recurrence: The Score" and "Acoustic Signatures: The Sound Design."
26. Sellors, "Collective Authorship in Film," 270.
27. "OSCAR-Nominated ARRIVAL screenwriter Eric Heisserer extended interview."

28. "Cinematographer Bradford Young Talks ARRIVAL."
29. Essman, "Contender—the Production Design of *Arrival*."
30. Hullfish, "ART OF THE CUT."
31. "Denis Villeneuve on How He Directed Arrival."
32. "DP/30: Arrival, Denis Villeneuve."
33. "DP/30: Arrival, Denis Villeneuve."
34. Hullfish, "ART OF THE CUT."
35. "The 50 Best Films of 2016 in the UK: The Full List," *Guardian*, November 29, 2016, https://www.theguardian.com/film/2016/nov/29/the-50-best-uk-films-of-2016-full-list.
36. Thomas Leitch notes that, by and large, Hitchcock avoided adapting renowned authors in order to assert his author-ity (*Film Adaptation and Its Discontents*, 239).
37. Chiang, *Stories of Your Life and Others*, 112.
38. Chiang, *Stories of Your Life and Others*, 123.
39. Quirk et al., *A Comprehensive Grammar of the English Language*, 228–229.
40. Quirk et al., *A Comprehensive Grammar of the English Language*, 198.
41. Here is another example of Chiang's use of tense and aspect: "I remember a conversation we'll have when you're in your junior year of high school. It'll be Sunday morning, and I'll be scrambling some eggs while you set the table for brunch" (Chiang, *Stories of Your Life and Others*, 129).
42. "Amy Adams on Denis Villeneuve's 'Arrival.'"
43. "Amy Adams on Denis Villeneuve's 'Arrival.'"
44. "Denis Villeneuve on How He Directed Arrival."
45. MacCabe, *True to the Spirit*, 7.
46. MacCabe, *True to the Spirit*, 7–8.
47. "Amy Adams on Denis Villeneuve's 'Arrival.'"
48. "DP/30: Arrival, Denis Villeneuve."
49. "OSCAR-Nominated ARRIVAL screenwriter Eric Heisserer extended interview."
50. See Bordwell's discussion of the "principles of causality, time, and space that are central to the 'protypical story'" (*Narration in the Fiction Film*, 39).

51. "DP/30: Arrival, Eric Heisserer."
52. "DP/30: Arrival, Denis Villeneuve."
53. "DP/30: Arrival, Denis Villeneuve."
54. In the DVD extra "Nonlinear Thinking: The Editing Process" and Hullfish, "ART OF THE CUT."
55. King, *Quality Hollywood*, 35.
56. King, *Quality Hollywood*, 101–105.
57. "OSCAR-Nominated ARRIVAL screenwriter Eric Heisserer extended interview."
58. "Denis Villeneuve ('Arrival') on Directing 'Poetic and Powerful' Sci-Fi Movie."

ARRIVAL AS HARD SOFT SCIENCE FICTION

1. Orozco, "Denis Villeneuve a gentiment viré Ridley Scott du tournage de Blade Runner 2049" (my translation).
2. Joshua Meyer, "Denis Villeneuve Thinks Christopher Nolan Is a 'Master' and Doesn't Consider Himself on That Level," SlashFilm, October 28, 2021, https://www.slashfilm.com/646585/denis-villeneuve-thinks-christopher-nolan-is-a-master-doesnt-consider-himself-on-that-level.
3. O'Falt, "Denis Villeneuve's Great Admiration for Christopher Nolan."
4. Brady, "'Dune' Director Denis Villeneuve Says He Was 'Blown Away.'"
5. Matt Rodgers, "Christopher Nolan Loved Denis Villeneuve's Dune, Calls It 'Compelling at Every Turn' and a 'Gift to Film Fans,'" Flickering Myth, October 26, 2021, https://www.flickeringmyth.com/2021/10/christopher-nolan-loved-denis-villeneuves-dune-calls-it-compelling-at-every-turn-and-a-gift-to-film-fans.
6. "Dune with Denis Villeneuve and Christopher Nolan (Ep. 323)."
7. "Is Denis Villeneuve the New Christopher Nolan?," Dirty Movies, October 9, 2021, https://www.dmovies.org/2021/10/09/denis-villeneuve-the-new-christopher-nolan.
8. Kevin Jagernauth, "Denis Villeneuve Talks Influence of

Ingmar Bergman & Steven Spielberg, Admiration for Christopher Nolan," The Playlist, December 22, 2017, https://theplaylist.net/denis-villeneuve-spielberg-nolan-20171222.

9. Longfellow, "Reproductive Futurism and the Woman Problem," 73.
10. Hoi-Tran Bui, "'Dune' Remake Will Be 'Star Wars for Adults,' Says Denis Villeneuve," SlashFilm, January 19, 2018, https://www.slashfilm.com/555747/dune-remake-star-wars-for-adults-denis-villeneuve.
11. Wright, "Genre Films and the Status Quo," 41–49; Telotte, *Science Fiction Film*, 43, 48, 95.
12. Westfahl, "Hard Science Fiction," 196.
13. Steele, "Hard Again," 4.
14. Westfahl, "Hard Science Fiction," 187.
15. Westfahl, "Hard Science Fiction," 189.
16. Buddy_Noone, "La hard science fiction au cinéma," Sens Critique, https://www.senscritique.com/liste/La_Hard_Science_au_cinema/819136; "Hard Science Fiction Movies," IMDb, https://www.imdb.com/list/ls066209068.
17. Westfahl, "Hard Science Fiction," 193.
18. Westfahl, "Hard Science Fiction," 196.
19. "DP/30: Arrival, Eric Heisserer."
20. Myriam Fontaine and Patrick Mullen, "Denis Villeneuve," *L'encyclopédie canadienne*, January 27, 2011, https://www.thecanadianencyclopedia.ca/fr/article/denis-villeneuve.
21. Grace Felder, "Everything We Know about the *Rendezvous with Rama* Movie," The Portalist, March 26, 2022, https://theportalist.com/rendezvous-with-rama-movie.
22. See Essman, "Contender—The Production Design of Arrival." See also "OSCAR-Nominated ARRIVAL screenwriter Eric Heisserer extended interview."
23. Don Kaye, "Interstellar: Kip Thorne and Jonathan Nolan Talk Science behind the Movie," Den of Geek, March 31, 2015, https://www.denofgeek.com/movies/interstellar-kip-thorne-and-jonathan-nolan-talk-science-behind-the-movie.

24. Coon, "Linguistics of *Arrival*." See also the following interview: "Jessica Coon: Linguistic Superstar," Government of Canada, September 24, 2018, https://www.noslangues-ourlanguages.gc.ca/fr/blogue-blog/jessica-coon-etoile-superstar-fra. See also "OSCAR-Nominated ARRIVAL screenwriter Eric Heisserer extended interview"; Gervais, "'Unstuck in Time.'"
25. "Principles of Time, Memory, and Language."
26. Westfahl, "Hard Science Fiction," 189.
27. Engle, "Of Hopis and Heptapods," 95; Sutton, "*Arrival*: Anthropology in Hollywood," 9–10.
28. Samuels, "Alien Tongues," 104.
29. In space operas like *Star Wars*, characters like Chewbacca are accompanied by other characters whose comprehension partly enables our own.
30. Chiang, *Stories of Your Life and Others*, 115.
31. Chiang, *Stories of Your Life and Others*, 137.
32. Chiang, *Stories of Your Life and Others*, 167–168.
33. Chiang, *Stories of Your Life and Others*, 116.
34. Sticchi, "From Spinoza to Contemporary Linguistics," 53; Gervais, "'Unstuck in Time'"; Jaunas, "Le monde vu par un autre"; Bréan, "Filiation et novum temporel."
35. "OSCAR-Nominated ARRIVAL screenwriter Eric Heisserer extended interview"; Norris, "Lovecraft and *Arrival*."
36. Nicol, "Humanities Fiction," 114; see also Gervais, "'Unstuck in Time.'"
37. Jaunas, "Le monde vu par un autre."
38. Sontag, "Imagination of Disaster."
39. Sobchack, *Screening Space*, 187, 191. *The Day the Earth Stood Still* also comprises two montage sequences, notably to describe the UFO's arrival, but they are not unified by the same media source.
40. *Arrival* is classically organized in four acts that, as in Kristin Thompson's methodology in *Storytelling in the New Hollywood*, can be identified through narrative turning points that affect the characters' motives and goals: the prologue

recounts Hannah's life and death; the first act sets up the basic premise, Louise's mission following the heptapods' arrival; the second act introduces the "complicating action" (the inability to communicate orally) that Louise attempts to resolve by focusing on written language; the third act, the "development," introduces a new parameter, Louise's visions; the final act, the climax, follows the announcement of General Shang's ultimatum.

41. The 1951 Dr. Mears describes geometry as "the basic and universal language," and the 1997 Ellie says that "mathematics is the only true universal language."
42. Nicol, "Humanities Fiction," 114, 117.
43. Sontag, "Imagination of Disaster."
44. Tan, *Emotion and the Structure of Narrative Film*, 94.
45. King, *Spectacular Narratives*, 8.

ARRIVAL AS A REFLECTION ON/OF COMMUNICATION

1. Wood, *Technoscience in Contemporary American Film*, 152–157.
2. Sobchack, 146–207.
3. Sutton, 8; Nicol, "Humanities Fiction," 109; Sticchi, 53.
4. Wood, *Technoscience in Contemporary American Film*, 16.
5. I am using David Bordwell's terminology from *Narration in the Fiction Film*. Extrinsic norms exist outside a given work and can be based as much on genre characteristics as on schemas of human perception; intrinsic norms are those that are developed within a given film (150–153).
6. Stam, introduction to *Literature and Film*, 16.
7. "Denis Villeneuve on How He Directed Arrival."
8. Sobchack, *Screening Space*, 199.
9. Buhler, "Postclassical Cinema and the Fraying of Narrative," 287.
10. Jaunas, "Le monde vu par un autre."
11. Kerbrat-Orecchioni, *Les Interactions verbales*, 137.
12. Sutton, "*Arrival*: Anthropology in Hollywood," 8.

13. "Amy Adams & Jeremy Renner—Arrival Exclusive Interview," YouTube video, uploaded by HeyUGuys, November 5, 2016, https://www.youtube.com/watch?v=r1OBFvZ5ugA.
14. "DP/30: Arrival, Denis Villeneuve."
15. Gervais, "'Unstuck in Time.'"
16. Mamula, "Denis Villeneuve, Film Theorist," 545.
17. Baudry, "Apparatus," 151.
18. Hatchuel, "Sérialité, spectralité, transfiction, revisionnage," 128.
19. Jaunas, "Le monde vu par un autre."
20. Griffiths, *Shivers down Your Spine*, 2.
21. Rose Biggin reminds us that immersion is "the action of immersing someone or something in liquid" (*Immersive Theatre and Audience Experience*, 27).
22. Bréan, "Filiation et novum temporel"; Bordwell, *Narration in the Fiction Film*, 39.
23. Jaunas, "Le monde vu par un autre."
24. Marks, *Skin of the Film*, xiv–xv; Sobchack, *Carnal Thoughts*, 60.
25. Griffiths, *Shivers down Your Spine*, 2.
26. Roche, *Meta in Film and Television Series*, 107–112.
27. Limoges, "La métalepse au cinéma," 132–139.
28. Hatchuel, "Sérialité, spectralité, transfiction, revisionnage," 128.
29. Mamula, "Denis Villeneuve, Film Theorist," 543.
30. Iser, *Act of Reading*, ix.
31. Lecercle, *Interpretation as Pragmatics*, 42.
32. Aumont et al., *Aesthetics of Film*, 144, 151.
33. Bordwell, *Narration in the Fiction Film*, 30, 59–62.
34. Chion, *Audio-Vision*, 5.
35. Bordwell, *Narration in the Fiction Film*, 72; Mamula, "Denis Villeneuve, Film Theorist," 545–546.
36. Jewitt, Bezemer, and O'Halloran, *Introducing Multimodality*, 2.
37. Iser, *Act of Reading*, 169.

38. Bordwell, *Figures Traced in Light*, 8.
39. "DP/30: Arrival, Eric Heisserer."
40. Buhler, "Postclassical Cinema and the Fraying of Narrative," 285.
41. Mamula, "Denis Villeneuve, Film Theorist," 550–551.

ARRIVAL AS AN EXPERIENCE OF TIME

1. Nicholas and Price, *Advanced Studies in Media*, 93; Whitaker, Ramsey, and Smith, *Media Writing*, 19–21.
2. These are some of the usual terms used by linguists to describe the progressive form. See Quirk et al., *Comprehensive Grammar of the English Language*, 198, 201.
3. Thompson and Bordwell, *Film History*, 673.
4. Bordwell, *Way Hollywood Tells It*, 100.
5. Buckland, "Introduction: Puzzle Plots," 6.
6. Bordwell, *Way Hollywood Tells It*, 80–81.
7. Buckland, "Mind-Game Film," 5.
8. Elsaesser, *Mind-Game Film*, 141–142.
9. Buckland, "Mind-Game Film," 7.
10. Buckland, "Mind-Game Film," 5.
11. Bordwell, "Arrival: When Is Now?"
12. Sticchi, "From Spinoza to Contemporary Linguistics," 52. See also Jaunas, "Le monde vu par un autre."
13. Bordwell, "Arrival: When Is Now?" See also Bréan, "Filiation et novum temporel."
14. Bordwell, "Arrival: When Is Now?"
15. Turim, *Flashbacks in Film*, 16, 189.
16. See also Langlet, *La Science-fiction*, 303–304.
17. Morris, *Cinema of Steven Spielberg*, 294–296; Gordon, *Empire of Dreams*, 231; Kendrick, *Darkness in the Bliss-Out*, 48–50.
18. Sticchi, "From Spinoza to Contemporary Linguistics," 61; Jaunas, "Le monde vu par un autre."
19. Hatchuel, "Sérialité, spectralité, transfiction, revisionnage," 130.

20. Elsaesser, *Mind-Game Film*, 142.
21. Mullarkey, "Gilles Deleuze," 187; quote from Deleuze, *Cinema 2*, 127.
22. Bergson cited in Deleuze, *Cinema 2*, 79.
23. Deleuze, *Cinema 2*, 70.
24. Deleuze, *Cinema 2*, 68, 89.
25. Buhler, "Postclassical Cinema and the Fraying of Narrative," 271, 285.
26. Deleuze, *Cinema 2*, 47.
27. Deleuze, *Cinema 2*, 75.
28. Deleuze, *Cinema 2*, 26–27.
29. Deleuze, *Cinema 2*, 80.
30. Deleuze, *Cinema 2*, 72–74.
31. Deleuze and Guattari, *Thousand Plateaus*, 266.
32. Deleuze, *Cinema 2*, 82.
33. Tarkovsky, *Sculpting in Time*, 57
34. Tarkovsky, *Sculpting in Time*, 79.
35. Deleuze, *Cinema 2*, 274.
36. Baudrillard, *Simulacra and Simulation*, 1, 21.
37. Deleuze, *Cinema 2*, 21, 23, 43.
38. Buhler, "Postclassical Cinema and the Fraying of Narrative," 286.
39. Buckland, "Mind-Game Film," 6.
40. Roche, "Death of the Subject."

ARRIVAL AS AN EXPERIENCE OF SPACE

1. Tuan, *Space and Place*, 10, 58.
2. Gardies, *L'Espace au cinéma*, 72.
3. Gardies, "Le paysage comme moment narratif," 142–143.
4. Lefebvre, "Entre lieu et paysage au cinéma," 132–134, 142–143.
5. Bréan, "Filiation et novum temporel."
6. Gervais, "'Unstuck in Time.'"
7. Augé, *Non-places*, 77–78.
8. Mayer, "Girl Power," 35.

9. Sobchack, *Screening Space*, 75, 283. Note that some UFOs are characterized by their irregular surface (*Independence Day*) or artificial lights (*Close Encounters of the Third Kind*, *E.T.*).
10. This shot recalls that of the stewardess bringing the pilots' food to the cockpit in *2001*.
11. Jaunas, "Le monde vu par un autre."
12. Burke, *Philosophical Enquiry into the Origin*, 53–56, 65–66.
13. Botting, *Gothic*, 3.
14. Sobchack, *Screening Space*, 285, 287.
15. Burke, *Philosophical Enquiry into the Origin*, 63–64.
16. Gelly and Roche, "Subjectivity and Cinematic Space," 166–170.
17. Some of the images on the monitor are, however, high-angle shots that cannot have been filmed by Captain Marks's camera.
18. See Clarke, *Cinematic City*; Mennel, *Cities and Cinema*; Lefebvre, *Landscape and Film*; Heath, "Narrative Space"; Bordwell, "Narration and Space," in *Narration in the Fiction Film*, 99–146.
19. Gaudin, *L'Espace cinématographique*, 9.
20. Gaudin, *L'Espace cinématographique*, 5 (my translation).
21. John Mullarkey explains that, in Deleuze's theory, "the moving images on screen (a quantity) extend to an off-screen set of images (a quality)" ("Gilles Deleuze," 181).
22. Bordwell defines "poetics" as the "general principles according to which the work is composed" (*Poetics of Cinema*, 12).
23. See Sophie Lécole Solnychkine, "Le Voile blanc où naissent les images."
24. "Denis Villeneuve ('Arrival') on Directing 'Poetic and Powerful' Sci-Fi Movie."

ARRIVAL AS A POLITICAL AND ETHICAL EXPERIENCE

1. Gómez-Muñoz, *Science Fiction Cinema in the Twenty-First Century*, 1, 3–4.

2. Yin and Xiao, "Hollywood's Global Strategy"; Gómez-Muñoz, *Science Fiction Cinema in the Twenty-First Century*, 5.
3. Fleming, "Race and World Memory in *Arrival*," 247, 265.
4. Nicol, "Humanities Fiction," 120.
5. Zavota, "Given (No) Time," 193; Gómez-Muñoz, *Science Fiction Cinema in the Twenty-First Century*, 107.
6. Mayer, "Girl Power," 38.
7. Fleming, "Race and World Memory in *Arrival*," 254.
8. Fleming, "Race and World Memory in *Arrival*," 265.
9. Nicol, "Humanities Fiction," 123–124.
10. Nicol, "Humanities Fiction," 124.
11. Gómez-Muñoz, *Science Fiction Cinema in the Twenty-First Century*, 131.
12. Fleming, "Race and World Memory in *Arrival*," 263.
13. Longfellow, "Reproductive Futurism and the Woman Problem," 70.
14. Mayer, "Girl Power," 48.
15. "Amy Adams: 'Arrival' Is a Mom Telling the Story of Her Life."
16. Chiang, *Stories of Your Life and Others*, 112.
17. "DP/30: Arrival, Denis Villeneuve."
18. Altman, *Film/Genre*, 72–77.
19. Basinger, "The Woman's Film," 13.
20. Doane, *Desire to Desire*, 3.
21. Doane, *Desire to Desire*, 4.
22. Clover, *Men, Women, and Chain Saws*, 53, 181, 217.
23. Doane, *Desire to Desire*, 122; quotes from 19.
24. Doane, *Desire to Desire*, 181.
25. Thornham, "'Hatred So Intense.'"
26. Gaudreault and Jost, *Cinéma et récit II*, 130.
27. The few scenes without Louise are typically brief and edited into short sequences, as if to show us: "Here's what going on in the male characters' lives." These include the military personnel studying TV and satellite images; Agent Halpern conversing with his Australian counterpart; Weber, Halpern,

and Kettler discussing Louise's health; and Marks speaking to his wife.

28. Merrick, "Gender in Science Fiction," 241.
29. Merrick, "Gender in Science Fiction," 248.
30. Kac-Vergne, *Masculinity in Contemporary Science Fiction Cinema*, 1, 5–7; Mayer, "Girl Power," 32.
31. Cornea, *Science Fiction Cinema*, 160.
32. Bordwell, "Arrival: When Is Now?"; Langlet, *La Science-fiction*, 270.
33. "DP30: The Oral History of Hollywood with Eric Heisserer."
34. Mayer, "Girl Power," 40.
35. Mayer, "Girl Power," 33, 36.
36. Silverman, *Acoustic Mirror*, 39.
37. "Denis Villeneuve on How He Directed Arrival."
38. Luce Irigaray famously described hysteria as "that privileged dramatization of female sexuality" (*Speculum of the Other Woman*, 60). For a critique of the essentialist collapsing of notions like "female intuition" and "feminist ethics," see Borgerson, "Why Feminist Ethics?," 118.
39. Fleming and Brown, "Through a (First) Contact Lens Darkly," 352.
40. I am here referring to Bordwell's and Thompson's writings on the hero of classical narration (Bordwell, *Narration in the Fiction Film*, 164; Thompson, *Storytelling in the New Hollywood*, 37).
41. Tasker, *Working Girls*, 69. See also Cornea, *Science Fiction Cinema*, 160–169.
42. Cornea, *Science Fiction Cinema*, 162.
43. Duden, *Disembodying Women*, 9–10.
44. Carruthers, "Temporality, Reproduction and the Not-Yet," 326.
45. Young, "Pregnant Embodiment."
46. Carruthers, "Temporality, Reproduction and the Not-Yet," 337.
47. See, for instance, Gorman and Kmec, "We (Have to) Try Harder."

48. Fleming and Brown, "Through a (First) Contact Lens Darkly," 355.
49. Ricœur, *Oneself as Another*, 172.
50. Taylor, *Sources of the Self*, 66.
51. Gervais, "'Unstuck in Time'"; Bréan, "Filiation et novum temporel."
52. Krzych, "Alternating Influences."
53. Fleming and Brown, "Through a (First) Contact Lens Darkly," 361.
54. Sticchi, "From Spinoza to Contemporary Linguistics," 50.
55. Sticchi, "From Spinoza to Contemporary Linguistics," 57–58.
56. Zavota, "Given (No) Time," 195, 202.
57. Zavota, "Given (No) Time," 202.
58. Longfellow, "Reproductive Futurism and the Woman Problem," 66.
59. Hurley, *Consciousness in Action*, 401.
60. Taylor, *Sources of the Self*, 69, 71.
61. "That Untranslated 'Arrival' Line Between Banks and Shang Is Finally Revealed."
62. Jaunas, "Le monde vu par un autre."
63. Levinas, *Totality and Infinity*, 21.
64. Levinas, *Totality and Infinity*, 79, 43.
65. Levinas, *Totality and Infinity*, 25–26.
66. Levinas, *Totality and Infinity*, 206–207.
67. Levinas, *Totality and Infinity*, 49.
68. Levinas, *Totality and Infinity*, 53, 102.
69. Levinas, *Totality and Infinity*, 51.
70. Levinas, *Totality and Infinity*, 40.
71. Levinas, *Totality and Infinity*, 101, 213.
72. Levinas, *Totality and Infinity*, 43, 75.
73. Longfellow, "Reproductive Futurism and the Woman Problem," 66, 70.
74. Levinas, "Substitution," 92.
75. Longfellow, "Reproductive Futurism and the Woman Problem," 71.
76. Levinas, *Éthique et infini*, 62 (my translation).

77. Jaunas, “Le monde vu par un autre.”
78. Ricœur, *Oneself as Another*, 140.
79. Levinas, *Totality and Infinity*, 216.
80. Longfellow, “Reproductive Futurism and the Woman Problem,” 70.

CONCLUSION

1. David Robey, in the introduction to Umberto Eco’s *Open Work* (xi).

Filmography

Arrival. Directed by Denis Villeneuve. Written by Eric Heisserer, based on the short story "Story of Your Life" by Ted Chiang. With Amy Adams (Louise Banks), Jeremy Renner (Ian Donnelly), Forest Whitaker (Colonel Weber), Michael Stuhlbarg (Agent Halpern), Mark O'Brien (Captain Marks), Tzi Ma (General Shang), Abigail Pniowsky (eight-year-old Hannah), Julia Scarlett Dan (twelve-year-old Hannah), Jadyn Malone (six-year-old Hannah), and Frank Schorpion (Dr. Kettler). Produced by Dan Cohen, Dan Levine, and Shawn Levy. Music: Jóhann Jóhannsson. Cinematography: Bradford Young. Film editing: Joe Walker. Casting: Francine Maisler. Production design: Patrice Vermette. Costume design: Renée April. Supervising sound editor: Sylvain Bellemare. Senior special effects supervisor: Andy Antoine. Lava Bear Films, FilmNation Entertainment, 21 Laps Entertainment, Xenolinguistics (copyright holder), 2016. Distributed by Paramount Pictures in the United States and Canada.

Other Films by Denis Villeneuve

2024: *Dune: Part Two*
2021: *Dune: Part One*
2017: *Blade Runner 2049*
2015: *Sicario*
2013: *Enemy*
2013: *Prisoners*
2010: *Incendies*
2009: *Polytechnique*
2008: *Next Floor* (short)
2007: *Un cri au bonheur* (collective documentary)

2006: *The Art of Seduction*, season 1, episode 1, "120 Seconds to Be Elected"
2006: *120 Seconds to Be Elected* (short)
2000: *Maëlstrom*
1998: *Un 32 août sur terre*
1996: *Cosmos* (segment "Le Technétium")
1994: *Daniel Bélanger: Ensorcelée* (music video)
1994: *REW FFWD* (documentary short)

Documentaries and Video Interviews

"Acoustic Signatures: The Sound Design." *Arrival*. Blu-ray. Sony Pictures, 2017.

"Amy Adams: 'Arrival' Is a Mom Telling the Story of Her Life." *Hollywood Reporter*, November 23, 2016. YouTube video, https://www.youtube.com/watch?v=3CulyFD9N_0.

"Amy Adams on Denis Villeneuve's 'Arrival.'" *Variety*, December 16, 2016. YouTube video, https://www.youtube.com/watch?v=MdnZbubfsdA.

"Cinematographer Bradford Young Talks ARRIVAL," Desde Hollywood, November 8, 2016. YouTube video, https://www.youtube.com/watch?v=CHx_VMqpbME.

"Denis Villeneuve ('Arrival') on Directing 'Poetic and Powerful' Sci-Fi Movie." Interview by Zach Laws. Gold Derby, December 6, 2016. https://www.goldderby.com/article/2016/denis-villeneuve-interview-arrival-amy-adams.

"Denis Villeneuve on How He Directed Arrival." Jilloms, August 24, 2019. YouTube video, https://www.youtube.com/watch?v=CZ6HhFO-h-g.

"DP/30: Arrival, Denis Villeneuve." DP/30: The Oral History of Hollywood, December 5, 2016. YouTube video, https://www.youtube.com/watch?v=v3wV_h5X8Tg.

"DP/30: Arrival, Eric Heisserer." DP/30: The Oral History of Hollywood, December 6, 2016. YouTube video, https://www.youtube.com/watch?v=hSt66t3kpKk.

"Dune with Denis Villeneuve and Christopher Nolan (Ep. 323)." The Director's Cut. SoundCloud video, https://soundcloud

.com/thedirectorscut/dune-with-denis-villeneuve-and-christopher-nolan-ep-323.

"Eternal Recurrence: The Score." *Arrival*. Blu-ray. Sony Pictures, 2017.

"Nonlinear Thinking: The Editing Process." *Arrival*. Blu-ray. Sony Pictures, 2017.

"OSCAR-Nominated ARRIVAL Screenwriter Eric Heisserer Extended Interview." Science vs Cinema, December 19, 2016. YouTube video, https://www.youtube.com/watch?v=7bI4xA_Q7WA.

"Principles of Time, Memory, and Language." *Arrival*. Blu-ray. Sony Pictures, 2017.

"Xenolinguistics: Understanding *Arrival*." *Arrival*. Blu-ray. Sony Pictures, 2017.

Bibliography

Books by Ted Chiang

Stories of Your Life and Others. 2002. Picador, 2020.

Interviews

Brady, Erin. "'Dune' Director Denis Villeneuve Says He Was 'Blown Away' by 'Tenet,' Calls It a 'Masterpiece.'" Collider, October 23, 2021. https://collider.com/denis-villeneuve-calls-tenet-masterpiece-christopher-nolan.

Conover, Stuart. "That Untranslated 'Arrival' Line between Banks and Shang Is Finally Revealed." ScienceFiction.com, February 21, 2017. https://sciencefiction.com/2017/02/21/that-untranslated-arrival-line-between-banks-and-shang-is-revealed.

Essman, Scott. "Contender—The Production Design of *Arrival*." Below the Line, January 23, 2017. https://www.btlnews.com/awards/contender-production-design-arrival.

Hullfish, Steve. "ART OF THE CUT with Joe Walker, ACE, on 'Arrival.'" Provideo Coalition, November 30, 2016. https://www.provideocoalition.com/art-of-the-cut-joe-walker-arrival.

O'Falt, Chris. "Denis Villeneuve's Great Admiration for Christopher Nolan, and Why He Wants to Make 'Dune.'" Indiewire, December 22, 2017. https://www.indiewire.com/2017/12/denis-villenueve-influences-christopher-nolan-steven-spielberg-ingmar-bergman-1201904623.

Orozco, Edouard. "Denis Villeneuve a gentiment viré Ridley Scott du tournage de Blade Runner 2049." Premiere, December

1, 2017. https://www.premiere.fr/Cinema/Denis-Villeneuve-a-gentiment-vire-Ridley-Scott-du-tournage-de-Blade-Runner-2049.

Books and Scholarly Articles on *Arrival* and Other Films of Denis Villeneuve

Bordwell, David. "Arrival: When Is Now?" Observations on Film Art, November 23, 2016. http://www.davidbordwell.net/blog/2016/11/23/arrival-when-is-now.

Bréan, Simon. "Filiation et novum temporel: Le cas d'*Interstellar* et d'*Arrival*." *Res Futurae* 17 (2021). https://doi.org/10.4000/resf.8970.

Buhler, James. "Postclassical Cinema and the Fraying of Narrative." In *Theories of the Soundtrack*, 284–288. Oxford University Press, 2018.

Carruthers, Anne. "Temporality, Reproduction and the Not-Yet in Denis Villeneuve's *Arrival*." *Film-Philosophy* 22, no. 3 (2018): 321–339.

Chamberlain, Edward. "Rethinking the Monstrous: Gender, Otherness, and Space in Cinematic Storytelling of Arrival." *CLCCWeb: Comparative Literature and Culture* 21, no. 7 (2019).

Coon, Jessica. "The Linguistics of Arrival: Heptapods, Field Linguistics, and Universal Grammar." In *Language Invention for Linguistics Pedagogy*, edited by Jeffrey Punske, Amy Fountain, and Nathan Sanders, 32–48. Oxford University Press, 2020. https://jessica.lingspace.org/wp-content/uploads/2019/04/Coon-Arrival.pdf.

Engle, John. "Of Hopis and Heptapods: The Return of Sapir-Whorf." *ETC: A Review of General Semantics* 73, no. 1 (2016): 95–99.

English, Jeri, and Marie Pascal, eds. *ReFocus: The Films of Denis Villeneuve*. Edinburgh University Press, 2023.

Fleming, David H. "Race and World Memory in *Arrival*." *Science Fiction Film and Television* 13, no. 2 (2020): 247–267.

Fleming, David H., and William Brown. "Through a (First) Contact Lens Darkly: *Arrival*, Unreal Time and Chthulucinema." *Film-Philosophy* 22, no. 3 (2018): 340–363.

Gelly, Christophe, and David Roche. "Subjectivity and Cinematic Space in *Blade Runner 2049*." In English and Pascal, *ReFocus*, 161–177.

Gervais, Bertrand. "'Unstuck in Time': L'arrachement au temps dans l'imaginaire de la fin contemporain. Arrival de Denis Villeneuve." *Monitorer le présent. L'écran à l'heure du soupçon*, no. 2 (2022). https://archiverlepresent.org/article-dun-cahier/unstuck-time-larrachement-au-temps-dans-limaginaire-de-la-fin-contemporain.

Hatchuel, Sarah. "Sérialité, spectralité, transfiction, revisionnage: (faire) revivre une fiction à l'écran." HDR dissertation, Université Paris-Diderot, 2018.

Jaunas, Vincent. "Le monde vu par un autre: L'identification des limites dans *Premier Contact* (*Arrival*, Denis Villeneuve, 2016)." *Miranda*, no. 22 (2021). https://doi.org/10.4000/miranda.37194.

Krzych, Scott. "Alternating Influences: Sublimation in Time-Travel Cinema." *World Picture*, no. 13 (2018). https://www.academia.edu/37307781/Alternating_Influences_Sublimation_in_Time_Travel_Cinema.

Longfellow, Brenda. "Reproductive Futurism and the Woman Problem in the Films of Denis Villeneuve." In English and Pascal, *ReFocus*, 59–75.

Mamula, Tijana. "Denis Villeneuve, Film Theorist; or, Cinema's Arrival in a Multilingual World." *Screen* 59, no. 4 (2018): 542–551.

Mayer, Sophic. "Girl Power: Back to the Future of Feminist Science Fiction with *Into the Forest* and *Arrival*." *Film Quarterly* 7, no. 3 (2017): 32–42.

Nicol, Bran. "Humanities Fiction: Translation and 'Transplanetarity' in Ted Chiang's 'The Story of Your Life' and Denis Villeneuve's *Arrival*." *American, British, and Canadian Studies* 32, no. 1 (2019): 107–126.

Noletto, Israel A. C., and Sebastião A. T. Lopes. "Heptapod B and the Paradox of Foreknowledge: Confronting Literature and Its Filmic Adaptation." *Arcadia* 54, no. 1 (2019): 86–100.

Norris, Duncan. "Lovecraft and *Arrival*: The Quiet Apocalypse." *Lovecraft Annual*, no. 11 (2017): 110–117.

Sticchi, Francesco. "From Spinoza to Contemporary Linguistics: Pragmatic Ethics in Denis Villeneuve's *Arrival*." *Canadian Journal of Film Studies / Revue canadienne d'études cinématographiques* 27, no. 2 (2018): 48–65.

Sutton, David. "*Arrival*: Anthropology in Hollywood." *Anthropology Today* 34, no. 1 (2018): 7–10.

Zavota, Gina. "Given (No) Time: A Derridean Reading of Denis Villeneuve's *Arrival*." *Film-Philosophy* 24, no. 2 (2020). https://doi.org/10.3366/film.2020.0138.

Film Studies

Altman, Rick. *Film/Genre*. BFI, 1999.

Aumont, Jacques, Alain Bergala, Michel Marie, and Marc Vernet. *Aesthetics of Film*. 1983. Translated and revised by Richard Neupert. University of Texas Press, 1992.

Basinger, Jeanine. "The Woman's Film: When Women Wept." In *Hollywood's America: Twentieth-Century America through Film*, edited by Steven Mintz and Randy Roberts, 163–169. Wiley-Blackwell, 2010.

Baudry, Jean-Louis. "The Apparatus: Metapsychological Approaches to the Impression of Reality in Cinema." 1975. Translated by Jean Andrews and Bernard Augst. In *Narrative, Apparatus, Ideology*, edited by Philip Rosen, 219–318. Columbia University Press, 1986.

Bordwell, David. *Figures Traced in Light: On Cinematic Staging*. University of California Press, 2005.

Bordwell, David. *Narration in the Fiction Film*. University of Wisconsin Press, 1985.

Bordwell, David. *Poetics of Cinema*. Routledge, 2007.

Bordwell, David. *The Way Hollywood Tells It: Story and Style in Modern Movies*. University of California Press, 2006.

Buckland, Warren. "Introduction: Puzzle Plots." In *Puzzle Films: Complex Storytelling in Contemporary Cinema*, edited by Buckland, 1–12. Wiley-Blackwell, 2009.

Buckland, Warren. "The Mind-Game Film: Provenance of a Concept." In Elsaesser, *The Mind-Game Film*, 4–10.

Chion, Michel. *Audio-Vision: Sound on Screen*. 1990. Translated by Claudia Gorbman. Columbia University Press, 1994.

Clarke, David B., ed. *The Cinematic City*. Routledge, 1997.

Clover, Carol J. *Men, Women, and Chain Saws: Gender in the Modern Horror Film*. Princeton University Press, 2015.

Cornea, Christine. *Science Fiction Cinema: Between Fantasy and Reality*. Rutgers University Press, 2007.

Deleuze, Gilles. *Cinema 2: The Time-Image*. 1985. Translated by Hugh Tomlinson and Robert Galeta. University of Minnesota Press, 1989.

Doane, Mary Ann. *The Desire to Desire: The Woman's Film of the 1940s*. Indiana University Press, 1987.

Elsaesser, Thomas. "The Mind-Game Film." In *Puzzle Films: Complex Storytelling in Contemporary Cinema*, edited by Warren Buckland, 13–41. Wiley-Blackwell, 2009.

Elsaesser, Thomas. *The Mind-Game Film: Distributed Agency, Time Travel, and Productive Pathology*. Edited by Warren Buckland, Dana Polan, and Seung-hoon Jeong. Routledge, 2021.

Elsaesser, Thomas. "A Retrospect: The Film Director as Auteur—Artist, Brand Name or Engineer?" 1995. http://www.thomas-elsaesser.com/images/stories/pdf/elsaesser_the_author_a_retrospect.pdf (site discontinued).

Gardies, André. *L'espace au cinéma*. Méridiens Klincksieck, 1993.

Gardies, André. "Le Paysage comme moment narratif." In *Les Paysages du cinéma*, edited by Jean Mottet, 141–153. Champ Vallon, 1999.

Gaudin, Antoine. *L'Espace cinématographique: Esthétique et dramaturgie*. Armand Colin, 2015.

Gaudreault, André, and François Jost. *Cinéma et récit II : Le récit cinématographique*. Nathan, 1990.

Gómez-Muñoz, Pablo. *Science Fiction Cinema in the Twenty-First Century: Transnational Futures, Cosmopolitan Concerns.* Routledge, 2022.

Gordon, Andrew M. *Empire of Dreams: The Science Fiction and Fantasy Films of Steven Spielberg.* Rowman & Littlefield, 2008.

Griffiths, Allison. *Shivers down Your Spine: Cinema, Museums, and the Immersive View.* Columbia University Press, 2008.

Haskell, Molly. *From Reverence to Rape: The Treatment of Women in the Movies.* University of Chicago Press, 1987.

Heath, Stephen. "Narrative Space." *Screen* 17, no. 3 (1976): 68–112.

Kac-Vergne, Marianne. *Masculinity in Contemporary Science Fiction Cinema: Cyborgs, Troopers and Other Men of the Future.* I. B. Tauris, 2017.

Kendrick, James. *Darkness in the Bliss-Out: A Reconsideration of the Films of Steven Spielberg.* Bloomsbury, 2014.

King, Geoff. *Quality Hollywood: Markers of Distinction in Contemporary Studio Film.* I. B. Tauris, 2016.

King, Geoff. *Spectacular Narratives: Hollywood in the Age of the Blockbuster.* I. B. Tauris, 2000.

Lécole Solnychkine, Sophie. "*Le Voile blanc où naissent les images.* Poe, Lovecraft, Carpenter: Résurgences figuratives." In *Edgar Poe et ses motifs à l'écran*, edited by David Roche and Vincent Souladié, 47–63. Presses Universitaires de Rennes, 2023.

Lefebvre, Martin. "Entre lieu et paysage au cinéma." *Poétique*, no. 130 (2002): 131–161.

Lefebvre, Martin. *Landscape and Film.* Routledge, 2007.

Leitch, Thomas. *Film Adaptation and Its Discontents: From* Gone with the Wind *to* The Passion of Christ. Johns Hopkins University Press, 2007.

Limoges, Jean-Marc. "La Métalepse au cinéma: Aux frontières de la transgression." *Cinergie*, no. 1 (2012): 126–144.

MacCabe, Colin, ed. *True to the Spirit: Film Adaptation and the Question of Fidelity.* Oxford University Press, 2011.

Marks, Laura U. *The Skin of the Film: Intercultural Cinema, Embodiment, and the Senses.* Duke University Press, 2000.

Mennel, Barbara. *Cities and Cinema*. 2008. Routledge, 2019.

Morris, Nigel. *The Cinema of Steven Spielberg: Empire of Light*. Wallflower Press, 2007.

Mullarkey, John. "Gilles Deleuze." In *Film: Theory and Philosophy: The Key Thinkers*, edited by Felicity Colman, 179–189. Acumen, 2009.

Roche, David. "The Death of the Subject in David Lynch's *Lost Highway* and *Mulholland Drive*." *E-rea* 2, no. 2 (2004). https://doi.org/10.4000/erea.432.

Roche, David. *Meta in Film and Television Series*. Edinburgh University Press, 2022.

Sellors, C. Paul. "Collective Authorship in Film." *Journal of Aesthetics and Art Criticism* 65, no. 3 (2007): 264–271.

Silverman, Kaja. *The Acoustic Mirror: The Female Voice in Psychoanalysis and Cinema*. Indiana University Press, 1988.

Sobchack, Vivian. *Carnal Thoughts: Embodiment and Moving Image Culture*. University of California Press, 2004.

Sobchack, Vivian. *The Limits of Infinity: The American Science Fiction Film 1950–75*. A. S. Barnes, 1980.

Sobchack, Vivian. *Screening Space: The American Science Fiction Film*. Rutgers University Press, 1997.

Sontag, Susan. "The Imagination of Disaster." *Commentary*, October 1965. https://www.commentary.org/articles/susan-sontag/the-imagination-of-disaster.

Stam, Robert. "Introduction: The Theory and Practice of Adaptation." In *Literature and Film: A Guide to the Theory and Practice of Film Adaptation*, edited by Robert Stam and Alessandra Raengo, 1–52. Blackwell, 2005.

Steele, Allen. "Hard Again." *New York Review of Science Fiction*, no. 46 (1992): 1, 3–5.

Tan, Ed S. *Emotion and the Structure of Narrative Film: Film as an Emotion Machine*. Translated by Barbara Fasting. Routledge, 1996. Reprinted 2011.

Tarkovsky, Andrey. *Sculpting in Time: Reflections on the Cinema*. 1986. Translated by Kitty Hunter-Blair. University of Chicago Press, 1989.

Tasker, Yvonne. *Working Girls: Gender and Sexuality in Popular Cinema*. Routledge, 1998.

Telotte, J. P. *Science Fiction Film (Genres in American Cinema)*. Cambridge University Press, 2001.

Thompson, Kristin. *Storytelling in the New Hollywood: Understanding Classical Narrative Technique*. Harvard University Press, 1999.

Thompson, Kristin, and David Bordwell. *Film History: An Introduction*. 1994. McGraw-Hill Higher Education, 2010.

Thornham, Sue. "'A Hatred So Intense . . .': *We Need to Talk about Kevin*, Feminism and Women's Cinema." *SEQUENCE: Media, Film and Music* 2, no. 1 (2013). https://reframe.sussex.ac.uk/sequence/files/2013/10/SEQUENCE-2.12013.pdf.

Turim, Maureen. *Flashbacks in Film: Memory and History*. 1989. Routledge, 2013.

Westfahl, Gary. "Hard Science Fiction." In *A Companion to Science Fiction*, edited by David Seed, 187–201. Blackwell, 2005.

Wood, Aylish. *Technoscience in Contemporary American Film*. Manchester University Press, 2002.

Wright, Judith Hess. "Genre Films and the Status Quo." In *Film Genre Reader II*, edited by Barry Keith Grant, 41–49. University of Texas Press, 1995.

Yin, Hong, and Zhiwei Xiao. "Hollywood's Global Strategy and the Future of Chinese Cinema." In *East Asian Cinemas: Regional Flows and Global Transformations*, edited by Vivian P. Y. Lee, 33–57. Palgrave Macmillan, 2011.

General Theory and Criticism

Augé, Marc. *Non-places: Introduction to an Anthropology of Supermodernity*. 1992. Translated by John Howe. Verso, 1995.

Baudrillard, Jean. *Simulacra and Simulation*. 1981. Translated by Sheila Faria Glaser. University of Michigan Press, 1994.

Biggin, Rose. *Immersive Theatre and Audience Experience: Space, Game and Story in the Work of Punchdrunk*. Palgrave Macmillan, 2017.

Borgerson, Janet. "Why Feminist Ethics?" In *Philosophy and*

Organization, edited by Campbell Jones and René ten Bos, 116–131. Routledge, 2007.

Botting, Red. *Gothic*. Routledge, 1996.

Burke, Edmund. *A Philosophical Enquiry into the Origin of Our Ideas of the Sublime and Beautiful*. 1757. Oxford University Press, 1990.

Deleuze, Gilles, and Félix Guattari. *A Thousand Plateaus: Capitalism and Schizophrenia*. 1980. Translated and with a foreword by Brian Massumi. Continuum, 2004.

Derrida, Jacques. *Given Time: I. Counterfeit Money*. 1991. Translated by P. Kamuf. University of Chicago Press, 1992.

Duden, Barbara. *Disembodying Women: Perspectives on Pregnancy and the Unborn*. Harvard University Press, 1993.

Eco, Umberto. *The Open Work*. 1962. Translated by Anna Cancogni, with an introduction by David Robey. Harvard University Press, 1989.

Gorman, Elizabeth, and Julie A. Kmec. "We (Have to) Try Harder: Gender and Required Work Effort in Britain and the United States." *Gender & Society* 21, no. 6 (2007): 828–856.

Haraway, D. J. *Staying with the Trouble: Making Kin in the Chthulucene*. Duke University Press, 2016.

Hurley, S. L. *Consciousness in Action*. Harvard University Press, 1998.

Irigaray, Luce. *Speculum of the Other Woman*. 1974. Translated by Gillian C. Gill. Cornell University Press, 1985.

Iser, Wolfgang. *The Act of Reading: A Theory of Aesthetic Response*. Johns Hopkins University Press, 1978.

Jewitt, Carey, Jeff Bezemer, and Kay O'Halloran. *Introducing Multimodality*. Routledge, 2016.

Kerbrat-Orecchioni, Catherine. *Les Interactions verbales Tome 1*. Armand Colin, 1990.

Lacan, Jacques. *The Seminar of Jacques Lacan*. Book 7: *The Ethics of Psychoanalysis 1959–1960*. 1986. Edited by Jacques Alain Miller and translated by Dennis Porter. W. W. Norton, 1992.

Langlet, Irène. *La Science-fiction: Lecture et poétique d'un genre littéraire*. Armand Colin, 2006.

Lecercle, Jean-Jacques. *Interpretation as Pragmatics*. Macmillan, 1999.

Levinas, Emmanuel. *Éthique et infini*. Fayard, Radio France, 1982.

Levinas, Emmanuel. *Totality and Infinity: An Essay on Exteriority*. 1961. Translated by Alphonso Lingis. Kluwer Academic, 1991.

Levinas, Emmanuel. "Substitution." 1968. In *Basic Philosophical Writings*, edited by Adriaan T. Peperzak, Simon Critchley, and Robert Bernasconi, 79–96. Indiana University Press, 1996.

Merrick, Helen. "Gender in Science Fiction." In *The Cambridge Companion to Science Fiction*, edited by Edward James and Farah Mandlesohn, 241–252. Cambridge University Press, 2003.

Nicholas, Joe, and John Price. *Advanced Studies in Media*. Thomas Nelson & Sons, 1998.

Quirk, Randolph, Sidney Greenbaum, Geoffrey Leech, and Jan Svartvik. *A Comprehensive Grammar of the English Language*. Longman, 1985.

Ricœur, Paul. *Oneself as Another*. 1990. Translated by Kathleen Blamey. University of Chicago Press, 1992.

Samuels, David. "Alien Tongues." In *E. T. Culture: Anthropology in Outerspaces*, edited by Debbora Battaglia, 94–129. Duke University Press, 2005.

Spinoza, Benedict de. *Ethics Demonstrated in Geometrical Order*. 1913. Edited by Matthew J. Kisner and translated by Michael Silverthorne and Matthew J. Kisner. Cambridge University Press, 2018.

Taylor, Charles. *Sources of the Self: The Making of the Modern Identity*. Harvard University Press, 1989.

Tuan, Yi-Fu. *Space and Place: The Perspective of Experience*. University of Minnesota Press, 1977.

Whitaker, Richard, Janet E. Ramsey, and Ronald D. Smith. *Media*

Writing: Print, Broadcast, and Public Relations. 2004. 4th ed. Routledge, 2012.

Young, Iris Marion. "Pregnant Embodiment: Subjectivity and Alienation." In *On Female Body Experience: "Throwing Like a Girl" and Other Essays*, 46–61. Oxford University Press, 2005.

Index

MIX
Papier | Fördert gute Waldnutzung
FSC® C083411

Zeitfracht Medien GmbH
Ferdinand-Jühlke-Straße 7
99095 Erfurt, Deutschland
produktsicherheit@kolibri360.de